CONTENTS

All the photographs in this book are by Rajendra Shaw, except where indicated.

© Oxfam 1991

Designed by Oxfam Design Department
OX:72/MJ/91
Printed by Oxfam Print Unit
Published by Oxfam
274 Banbury Road, Oxford OX2 7DZ

ISBN 085598 153 9

IND

PATHS TO DEVELOPMENT

Julia Cleves Mosse

2

Facts and Figures

Area:	3,288,000 square kms.
Population:	844 million (provisional 1991).
Population growth rate:	2.1 (average annual growth rate 1981-91).
Population density:	256 per square km [UK 233 per square km].
Life expectancy at birth:	58 years (1988).
Infant mortality:	97 per 1000 live births (1988).
1 Doctor for every:	2,520 people (1984) [UK 1 doctor for every 650 people].
Literacy:	Men 64%; women 39% (1991).
GNP per capital:	$340 (1988).
Principle exports:	Value $14.6 billion (1988). Tea, leather, gemstones, marine products, iron ore, chemicals, cotton goods, jute, engineering goods and silk.
Principle imports:	Value $ 22.5 billion (1988). Petroleum products, fertilisers, iron and steel.
Main trading partners:	USSR, EC, Japan, USA.
Currency:	The rupee (Rs). Average value against the pound in 1990 Rs35 = £1. This is the figure that has been used for conversion from rupees to sterling throughout this report.

Acknowledgments

I would like to thank all the Oxfam staff in India and on the Asia desk who were so helpful in organising project visits, and commenting on various drafts of the manuscript. Particular thanks are due to Oxfam's project partners in India for giving their time to show us the work they are doing, and to all the people who told me their stories and let Rajendra Shaw photograph them. Finally, I'd like to give special thanks to Oxfam's team in Bangalore — Barbie, Sandra, Gunal, Xavier, Syed, Sheelu, Vimal, Roland, Meru and David — for all that they have taught me about India in the last three years.

Julia Cleves Mosse
Bangalore

> *'India is a cultural unity amidst diversity, a bundle of contradictions held together by strong but invisible threads.'*
>
> Jawaharlal Nehru

PEOPLE

The people of India have over 1,500 different mother tongues, an indication of the enormous diversity of life on the Indian subcontinent. The 15 major languages that make up the 'official' languages of India each have their own script, literary tradition, and contemporary writers and poets. Hindi and Bengali are the fifth and sixth most spoken languages in the world. Each language is an expression of a way of life and a unique history; few countries in the world can boast such variety or so lively a contemporary culture as India.

India's wealth of differences has been maintained partly by its large rural population and partly by its size. People living in India's southern-most state live as far away from their capital as people in Athens live from London. A trip from Bombay to Delhi is much like travelling from Rome or Madrid to London. India's villages – some 575,000 of them in the 1981 census – have until very recently been isolated rural communities. Only in the last two decades has anything like a modern cultural mainstream (cars, fashions, popular music and so on) begun to emerge. Consequently, the differences among rural people from one end of India to the other are considerable. Clothing, food, customs and appearance change significantly from Jammu and Kashmir to Kerala, or from Gujarat to Assam. At the same time, the material expectations of India's middle-class city population have much in common with those of people in the West. Yet, as Nehru explained, India remains a whole, bound together by ancient cultural roots, by the caste system, and by its living democratic tradition.

India's estimated population in 1991 of over 840 million makes it the second most populous nation in the world, although its population density is no higher than many European countries. Indians now constitute almost one sixth of the global population; the populations of most of India's states are larger than those of many countries in the world. Uttar Pradesh, for example, India's most populous state, has roughly the same population as Japan – currently ranked seventh in the world. India's commitment to education and industry has given the country one of the biggest and most skilful workforces in the world, second only in size to those of the US and USSR. This has also been reflected in the rapid urbanisation of India. Despite the fact that only a quarter of Indians live in towns and cities, the urban population is as big as that of the United States.

PHYSICAL FEATURES

India is a country of many different landscapes. Its great size embraces much diversity; it spans 3,200 kilometres from the snowy Himalayan heights of Jammu and Kashmir to semi-tropical Kanyakumari in the extreme south, and 2,700 kilometres from the hot, dry plains of Gujarat to the hills, oil fields and tea estates of Assam in the east. India's coastline is more than 6,400 kilometres long, while to the North, East and West it shares borders with six other countries: Pakistan, Nepal, China, the Soviet Union, Burma, Bhutan and Bangladesh.

Geographers explain India's landscape by pointing to seven geographical regions – the mountains in the north (the Great Himalaya); the Ganga plain, where the great River Ganges flows; the central highlands, many of which are still under thick forest cover; the Thar desert of Rajasthan; Peninsular India, the large part of India that protrudes into the sea which is edged with mountain chains; the coastal areas of West and East India; and the two sets of islands off the Indian coast, the Andaman and Nicobar Islands in the Bay of Bengal, and Lakshadweep in the Arabian Sea.

One of the most spectacular features of India's weather is the arrival of the monsoon. Indian farming, like British farming, relies largely on rain water; only 20 per cent of Indian farmland is watered from special irrigation projects. India has two monsoons, the south-west monsoon and the north-east monsoon, although the south-west monsoon is far and away the most important of the two, bringing 70 per cent of the country's annual rainfall. The south-west monsoon is also the more predictable; it usually arrives in India by around the first of June, and spreads northwards from Kerala so that by July the whole country is experiencing torrential rain. Monsoons bring with them an average annual rainfall of 125cm, although some parts of Rajasthan get as little as 15cm, and parts of the North East a massive 900cm a year.

The monsoon cycle creates distinct seasons. Once the rains have finished in September, India enjoys a cool, dry winter lasting from October to February. Winter may be a relative term, since the coolest month of the year is January, with an average temperature of between 12.5 C in the Punjab, and 25.5 C in Tamil Nadu. From the beginning of March the temperature rises rapidly, reaching scorching heights of up to 47 C in Delhi and other central and northern cities.

Parts of India regularly experience drought when the monsoon either misses them out altogether, or brings very little rain. Estimates suggest that 16 per cent of the country regularly fails to get enough water. Ironically, a similar proportion of India is often flooded during the monsoon, particularly parts of Assam and northern Bihar.

Terracing makes it possible to grow crops on the steep slopes of the Kumaon Hills, in Uttar Pradesh. These hills form the foothills of the Great Himalaya.
I A Simpson/FAO

The Ganges, one of the world's great rivers, rises in the Himalayas and flows across the Ganga plain out to the sea in the Bay of Bengal.

The forest of the Dangs. India's forest cover is rapidly disappearing; every year another 1.5 million hectares of forests are cleared.

A HISTORY OF INVASION

Independent India came into being in 1947, the culmination of a history that can be traced back some 5,000 years. India's rich natural resources – spices, indigo, silk, sugar, cotton, saltpetre, sandalwood and ivory – made it a target for invasion and colonisation by European powers from the fifteenth century onwards. But the history of invasion reaches back to the Aryans, Indo-Europeans who entered India from the north-west and overthrew the city-based Harappa civilisation around 3000 BC. Their hymns and poems are still recited in Hindu worship, giving India one of the oldest continual cultural traditions in the world. The Buddha's influence (c.567-487 BC) on Indian culture was largely confined to the North, though the great Buddhist Emperor Asoka (c.273-232 BC) extended his empire throughout Northern and Central India, writing his edicts on pillars and rocks wherever his power extended.

India's history until the fifteenth century is resplendent with mighty empires and dynasties that rose and fell, leaving some of the great buildings and art of the world behind them —the caves of Ajanta, Ellora, Sanchi and Sarnarth for example, created by the Gupta kings in the third century AD. From the eighth century onwards Muslim invasions began from the Middle East, although it was not until 1192 that Muslim power arrived on a more permanent basis when the first Sultan of Delhi established his court. In 1526 Babar, the first of the great Mughul emperors, arrived in India from Turkey, and the Mughuls retained power until the beginning of the eighteenth century, when their empire began to crumble. Their legacy, stemming from a great passion for building and for arts and literature, has proved a major influence on India. As the Muslim empire waned, European colonial power began to fill its place. Another of the major influences on contemporary India was taking shape.

Temples in Bhubeneswar, Orissa.

THE BRITISH IN INDIA

The history of the British Raj begins in 1600 when, on the last day of the year, a small group of men set up the East India Company, a trading company designed to exploit India's rich natural resources. At this point no one could have dreamed that India would one day become the 'Jewel in the Crown' of the British Empire. At first the British confined themselves to trade and commerce, but by 1757 when Robert Clive of the East India Company defeated the Nawab of Bengal in the Battle of Plassey, Britain's determination to maintain its highly profitable trading links meant that the East India Company had to extend its function to administration, beginning in 1764 with Bengal. The Company gradually extended its rule throughout the south and east and as far north as the Sutlej river. By the 1840s the Punjab, Sind and Kashmir had also been annexed. In 1858 the British Crown took over from the East India Company as ruler in India. The second half of the nineteenth century has been described as the 'imperial heyday' of the British in India.

What were the motives of the Empire builders? One potent motive was trade, and the hope that India would provide a large market for domestic products. Throughout the nineteenth century a belief in the moral superiority of Western civilisation came to dominate Britain's imperial policy. This ideology was expressed in slogans such as 'the inestimable benefits of civilisation'; it embraced a belief that scientific rationality would triumph over the naive and 'childlike' beliefs of Hinduism. (As one historian of the period has pointed out, a Victorian seriously believed that he was five times as good as other people because he travelled five times as fast.) Even among European intellectuals, there was an almost complete consensus that colonialism was a necessary evil, a necessary stage of maturation for some societies. Colonisers were seen not as self-seeking opportunists but as fulfilling a 'great moral duty...in India'.

Forty years after Independence, we look at British colonialism in India with different eyes. We can see the arrogance of the colonialist view that British rule was the consummation to which all Indian history had been moving, rather than one episode among many in that long history. Far from conferring 'inestimable benefits', Mahatma Gandhi stated in 1930 that, 'The British Government has ruined India economically, politically, culturally and spiritually...We hold it to be a crime against man and God to submit any longer to a rule that has caused this fourfold disaster to our country.' Indian leaders were under no illusion that the 'great moral duty' was also fuelled by self-interest. Winston Churchill himself pointed out that one in five Britishers were maintained by Indian resources, and he recognised that the control of India was almost a matter of life and death for the British Empire.

Indian writers such as Ashis Nandy have explored the idea that colonialism has its profoundest effects not in geographical and political terms, but on the minds of both the colonised and the colonisers. It was for this reason that Mahatma Gandhi implicitly defined his ultimate goal as the liberation of the British from the history and psychology of British colonialism. He turned the moral superiority argument on its head; one of the driving forces in the fight for independence was his belief in the moral and cultural superiority of the oppressed.

'The jewel in the Crown': print from the heyday of the British Raj.
The Hulton Deutsch Collection

Bombay Green, 1767.
The Hulton Deutsch Collection

THE STRUGGLE FOR INDEPENDENCE

India's struggle for independence really began in the second half of the nineteenth century. By then the infrastructure of British imperialism – railways, a postal and telegraph system and national newspapers – had begun to unite the country and foster something of a national consciousness. The Englishman A.O. Hume who was instrumental in setting up the Indian National Congress (INC), the forerunner of the current Congress party, in 1885 described the mood of the times: 'The ferment due to the creation of Western ideas, education, inventions and appliances was at work...A safety valve for the escape of great and growing forces was urgently needed.' Members of the INC, under the leadership of the moderate G.K.Gokhale and the more radical B.G.Tilak, put forward moderate proposals to the British Government, but year after year most of the demands were rejected. The Government dismissed it as representing only a 'microscopic minority' of Indians.

By 1905 the mood in India had changed so far that, when Bengal was partitioned into a Muslim east and Hindu west, there was a massive backlash, a boycott of British goods, and a ceremonial burning of Lancashire cotton. The communal tensions that were to lead to Partition were already present at this time. The Muslims, fearing that they would become an isolated minority in a Hindu state, formed in 1906 the Muslim League, initially in a spirit of loyalty to Britain and in opposition to the INC. The First World War had a major effect on British standing in India. It was seen for the first time as one among several approximately equal European powers. By 1916, Annie Besant, in an INC address, could state: 'India demands Home Rule...India is no longer on her knees for boons; she is on her feet for Rights'.

Mahatma Gandhi had returned to India from South Africa in 1915, and by 1919 had begun to influence the Nationalist movement. He pursued his policy of *satyagraha*, a form of protest 'which eschews violence absolutely as a matter of principle'. One of his first public actions was to call a *hartal*, a day when all work ceases, in protest at the Rowlatt Bills which allowed judges to try political cases without juries. The massacre at Amritsar happened in April 1919, when British troops shot at a peaceful crowd. Known in India as the Jallian Wallah Bagh tragedy, the official death toll was 379: unofficial estimates claim that almost 1000 people were killed. It was after Amritsar that Gandhi changed his attitude to British rule, declaring that 'cooperation in any shape or form with this satanic government is sinful'.

The 1920s saw the start of a civil disobedience movement, the arrest and imprisonment of Gandhi, and a lull in the Nationalist movement. The 1930s brought the launch of another civil disobedience movement. One of Gandhi's best known actions was his march to the coast at Dandi to make illicit salt in protest at the salt tax; the British responded swiftly, and by 1933 over 120,000 people had been arrested. India became increasingly difficult to govern. A massive wave of violent sabotage in 1942, Gandhi's 'Quit India' campaign, escalating violence between Hindus and Muslims, Jinnah's demand for a new sovereign state of Pakistan, and the outbreak of the Second World War put enormous strain on the British. By the end of the war, Britain was indeed ready to quit. Lord Mountbatten was sent out to India as Viceroy, and became convinced of the necessity of Partition. On 1 July 1947 the British Parliament passed the India Independence Bill, and on 15 August, India awoke to freedom.

Parliament building, New Delhi.

Gandhi's room, preserved as it was in his lifetime, Sabarnathi Ashram, Ahmedabad. Gandhi's ideas, emphasising simplicity, non-violence and the importance of village-level solutions are still of immense importance in India.

INDEPENDENT INDIA

1947: Jawaharlal Nehru, Prime Minister; Lord Mountbatten Governor-General. August/September: Partition: five and a half million people travelled each way over the new India-Pakistan border, and over a million between East Pakistan (now Bangladesh) and West Bengal. Many massacred in Punjab.

1948: 30 January Gandhi assassinated. Truce in Kashmir and accession of Kashmir to Indian Union.

1950: 26 January Constitution of Indian Union implemented. Indian National Planning Commission set up.

1951: First Five Year Plan inaugurated.

1955/6: Hindu Succession Act and Hindu Marriage Act improved women's legal status, allowing them to inherit property; divorce and alimony given legal basis.

1956: States Reorganisation Act passed.

1961: Portuguese possessions of Goa, Daman and Diu liberated.

1962: Indo-Chinese hostilities on the Tibetan frontiers.

1964: Death of Jawaharlal Nehru.

1965: Hostilities with Pakistan over Kashmir. Hindi proclaimed national language.

1966/7: Severe drought with major famine, particularly in Bihar.

1971: War with Pakistan. India recognises new state of Bangladesh.

1975: Declaration of Emergency, drastically curtailing political and individual rights.

1977: Emergency ends. Cyclone havoc in Andhra Pradesh and Tamil Nadu.

1984: Operation Blue Star: Indian troops enter Golden Temple in Amritsar. 31 October Indira Gandhi assassinated by bodyguards. Rajiv Gandhi becomes leader of the Congress party and Prime Minister. Bhopal disaster: death of several thousand people in one of the world's worst industrial accidents.

1987: Drought in many parts of India. Sri Lankan Accord; Indian Peace Keeping Force sent to Sri Lanka.

1989: General Election. Renewed violence in Kashmir. Indian Peace Keeping Force withdraws from Sri Lanka.

1990: V.P.Singh announces his decision to implement the report of the Mandal Commission which recommends reserving places for backward castes in education, training and government service. Anti-reservation riots sweep India. Hindu-Muslim conflict over a holy site in the city of Ayodhya. V.P. Singh resigns as Prime Minister and is replaced by Chandra Shekhar.

1991 Chandra Shekhar resigns as Prime Minister. General election called.

INDIA: A UNION OF STATES

Modern India is a federation of 25 states and 7 union territories, organised largely according to language. At Independence, in addition to the regions directly administered by the British, India still had over 360 semi-autonomous Princely states; Hyderabad was one of the largest with a population of 17 million, while the smallest consisted of only a few square kilometres. The movement for the creation of linguistic states was given a great spur by a man called Potti Sriramulu, who starved himself to death in 1952 in the cause of a Telegu-speaking state to be called Andhra. In 1956 there was a radical reorganisation of the states under the States Reorganisation Act and the modern map of India came into being. Since 1956 there have been some changes, and some new states created; Haryana for example was created in 1966 and Goa was recognised as a state in its own right in 1987.

Income per head varies from state to state in India, from a high Rs4000 a year in the Punjab, to as little as Rs1000-1500 in Tamil Nadu, Orissa, Madhya Pradesh, Bihar and some of the smaller North-Eastern States. This discrepancy is often an indication of the amount of modern industry or green revolution farming there is in the state.

The violence that has swept India in the last few years has attracted considerable media attention around the world. The tension in Jammu and Kashmir and in the Punjab, and the violence that has erupted around the Ayodhya issue have suggested how fragile a Union of both States and communities India actually is. But however strong the forces pulling India apart, there is an equal force resisting such fragmentation, and most Indians are saddened and alarmed by outbreaks of violence. There is a strong movement in India against communal violence and the fragmentation of the Union. The 'strong but invisible threads' that Nehru evoked continue for the time being to hold India together.

JAMMU AND KASHMIR
Area: 222,236 sq km
Population: 8m
Languages: Urdu, Kashmiri, Dogri, Ladhaki

HIMACHAL PRADESH
Area: 55,673 sq km
Population: 4m
Languages: Hindi Punjabi, Dogri

PUNJAB
Area: 50,362 sq km
Population: 20m
Languages: Punjabi, Hindi

HARYANA
Area: 44,212 sq km
Population: 16m
Languages: Hindi, Punjabi

RAJASTHAN
Area: 342,239 sq km
Population: 44m
Languages: Rajasthani, Hindi

GUJARAT
Area: 196,025 sq km
Population: 41m
Languages: Gujarati, Bhili, Marathi, Sindhi, Hindi

MAHARASHTRA
Area: 307,690 sq km
Population: 79m
Languages: Marathi, Gujarathi, Hindi, Gond

GOA, DAMAN AND DIU
Area: 3,814 sq km
Population: 1m
Languages: Konkani, Marathi, Gujarati, Portuguese.

KARNATAKA
Area: 191,791 sq km
Population: 45m
Languages: Kannada, Urdu, Tamil

KERALA
Area: 38,863 sq km
Population: 29m
Languages: Malayalam, Tamil

TAMIL NADU
Area: 130,058 sq km
Population: 56m
Languages: Tamil, Urdu, Telegu

ANDHRA PRADESH
Area: 275,086 sq km
Population: 66m
Languages: Telegu, Urdu, Tamil

MADHYA PRADESH
Area: 443, 646 sq km
Population: 66m
Languages: Hindi, Urdu

ORISSA
Area: 155,707 sq km
Population: 31m
Languages: Oriya, Kui, Sambalpuri

BIHAR
Area: 173,877 sq km
Population: 86m
Languages: Hindi, Urdu, Santali

UTTAR PRADESH
Area: 294,411 sq km
Population: 139m
Languages: Hindi, Urdu

WEST BENGAL
Area: 87,853 sq km
Population: 68m
Languages: Bengali, Hindi

Note: We have used the provisional figures from the 1991 census where these are available.

NORTH EASTERN STATES

ARUNACHAL PRADESH
Area: 83,743 sq km
Population: 0.6m
Languages: Tribal languages, Nepali

TRIPURA
Area: 10,486 sq km
Population: 2m
Languages: Bengali, Tripuri

MEGHALAYA
Area: 22,429 sq km
Population: 1m
Languages: English, Khasi

MANIPUR
Area: 22,327 sq km
Population: 1m
Languages: Manipuri, English, Tangkhul

MIZORAM
Area: 21,081 sq km
Population: 0.5m
Languages: Mizo, English

SIKKIM
Area: 7,096 sq km.
Population: 0.3m
Languages: Nepali, Lepcha, Bhutia

NAGALAND
Area: 16,579 sq km
Population: 0.8m
Languages: Nagamese, English, Nepali

ASSAM
Area: 78,523 sq km
Population: 22m
Languages: Assamese, Bodo, Bengali, Hindi

JAMMU & KASHMIR

HIMACHAL PRADESH

PUNJAB

Pakistan

HARYANA

Delhi •

China

Nepal

Bhutan

NORTH EASTERN STATES

UTTAR PRADESH

RAJASTHAN

BIHAR

Bangladesh

WEST BENGAL

Calcutta •

GUJARAT

Bhopal •

Ahmedabad •

MADHYA PRADESH

Myanmar
(formerly Burma)

ORISSA

MAHARASHTRA

Bombay •

• **Hyderabad**

ANDHRA PRADESH

GOA

KARNATAKA

Bangalore •

• **Madras**

Other Union territories:
Andaman and Nicobar Islands (population 0.2m)
Chandigarh (0.5 m)
Dadra and Nagar Havelli (0.1m)
Delhi (6m)
Lakshadweep (27 islands of the SW coast) (0.4m)
Pondicherry (0.6m)

KERALA

TAMIL NADU

Sri Lanka

POLITICS:
The largest democracy in the world

'WE THE PEOPLE OF INDIA
having solemnly resolved to constitute India into a
SOVEREIGN SOCIALIST, SECULAR, DEMOCRATIC REPUBLIC
AND to secure to all citizens, JUSTICE, social, economic and political;
LIBERTY of thought, expression, belief, faith and worship;
EQUALITY of status and opportunity; and to promote among them all
FRATERNITY assuring the dignity of the individual and the unity and
integrity of the nation; IN OUR CONSTITUENT ASSEMBLY this 26th day
of November 1949 DO HEREBY ADOPT, ENACT, AND GIVE TO
OURSELVES THIS CONSTITUTION.'
(As worded by the 42nd Amendment.)

O f all the countries that have emerged from colonial status in this century, India stands out as the largest, and arguably the most consistent example of democracy. When the revision of the electoral rolls was carried out in 1988, the electorate recorded was 450,378,862, and since then the voting age has been reduced to 18, adding a further 10-11 per cent to India's voting population.

India's political system operates within terms set down by the constitution. It borrows from political systems throughout the world, and uses the Westminster model of a central parliament, with two houses, the Lok Sabha (House of the People) and the Rajya Sabha (Council of States), in New Delhi. Each State also has its own Legislative Assembly.

India's Parliament has responsibility for issues such as defence, nuclear energy, railways, shipping, posts and telegraphs, banking and currency, and the Supreme and High Courts. The States, who receive their budgets from Parliament, are responsible for, among other things, public order, police, administration of justice, prisons, forests, fisheries, agriculture, education, and the protection of wild animals.

One unique feature of India's constitution is its special treatment of people who have traditionally been at a disadvantage, such as tribal people. Special seats are reserved for them in the legislative assemblies. The Lok Sabha reserves 78 seats for members of scheduled castes (ex-untouchables) and 41 seats for people from scheduled tribes. India's constitution says that 'the State shall promote with special care the educational and economic interests of the weaker sections of the people and in particular of the Scheduled Castes and the Scheduled Tribes, and shall protect them from social injustice and all forms of exploitation'. (Article 46.)

India has played a conspicuous political role during the last 40 years, regionally in South Asia, and internationally through its role in the Nonaligned Movement (the NAM, which Jawaharlal Nehru helped to found), the Commonwealth, and in its strong commitment to international institutions such as the United Nations. Its nonaligned position has enabled India to benefit from good political and economic relationships with the USSR, USA, and the EC countries.

Elections since Independence

India became independent on 15 August 1947, and proclaimed itself a Republic on 26 January 1950, when the Indian Constitution came into force. The first elections were held two years later, and since then there have been a total of nine General or Lok Sabha elections.

India, like Britain, has a first-past-the-post system of polling, and in all but two of the Lok Sabha elections (1967, 1989) this has resulted in clear majorities. Although Congress has never won 50 per cent of the vote, it has been the governing

The Indian Parliament consists of two Houses and a President Parliament deals with issues such as defence, energy, railways, shipping, post and telegraphs, banking and currency.

Rajya Sabha MP's voted in by the State Vidhan Sabhas

Lok Sabha MP's voted in at General Elections

The State Assemblies deal with issues such as public order, the Police, administration of justice (except supreme and high courts), prisons, forests, fisheries, agriculture, education and the protection of wild animals.

Members of the Legislative Assembly voted in at State-level elections

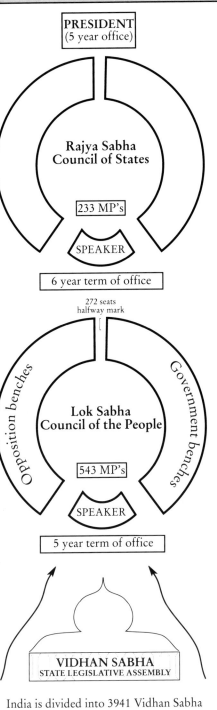

PRESIDENT
(5 year office)

**Rajya Sabha
Council of States**

233 MP's

SPEAKER

6 year term of office

272 seats
halfway mark

Opposition benches

Government benches

**Lok Sabha
Council of the People**

543 MP's

SPEAKER

5 year term of office

**VIDHAN SABHA
STATE LEGISLATIVE ASSEMBLY**

India is divided into 3941 Vidhan Sabha
constituencies. Each state has a
Vidhan Sabha, or State Legislative Assembly.
On average, 7 Vidhan Sabha constituencies
form one Lok Sabha constituency.

*Because there are still many
people in India who have never
been taught to read, symbols are a
vital part of election propaganda.
Here are two examples – the
hammer and sickle (Communist
Party) and the hand (Congress (I)
Party).*

party in India for most of the time. The only years in which Congress has not been in power were just after the Emergency in 1977, when the Janata Party won the general election on something of a protest vote, and more recently. The 1989 elections were regarded as a watershed in Indian politics, when V.P.Singh formed his government out of an alliance between his party, the Janata Dal, and the Communists and right-of-centre BJP. The political upheavals of the last few months of 1990 left India with another new Prime Minister, Chandra Sekhar, supported by a splinter group of the Janata Dal.

Election fever
November 1989

The coming election dominates everything; the excitement in the air is palpable. Almost tail to tail, autorickshaws, lorries and cars, decked out with banners, flags, election symbols and public address systems, cruise through urban streets. The rhythmic chant from one car is almost like Rap poetry: 'Ja-na-ta, Ja-na-ta, Ja-na-ta Dal'. A little later a Congress (I) lorry comes by, the windscreen almost entirely blocked by a huge portrait of Mrs. Gandhi; Nehru and Rajiv Gandhi are strapped to the sides. A group of musicians sitting in the back are singing political *ragas*, the words amplified out of recognition. One Monday morning a roundabout is decked out with Congress flags and banners. The next morning it has switched affiliation to Janata Dal. Overnight every available surface, trees, walls and houses, sprout political symbols daubed on with brush and paint. Symbols are a vital part of election propaganda in a country where many people cannot read. Each party is given a symbol by the election committee and it appears on the ballot paper. Parties are often known only by their symbol. Krishnan, a gardener from Bangalore, explained that his family and most of his caste community would vote for 'the hand' – in other words the Congress (I) party.

How do people view general elections? Do they feel their vote counts? Sunitha and Chandra are both secretaries, working in Bangalore. Sunitha summed up her feelings, 'You never really know whether elections are fair. Certainly in towns, where the population is literate, the outcome reflects the wishes of the voters, but in rural areas, which are after all the majority, I think votes can be bought and whole communities persuaded to vote one way or another.' Chandra discussed the outcome of the 1989 elections. 'I decided who to vote for on the basis of the programmes offered. I looked and saw which way the wind was blowing. There were lots of candidates in the last election – 24 on my ballot paper, many of them independent. You had to look through two sheets of paper to find the candidate you wanted. As far as most people were concerned, though, it was just a competition between Janata Dal and Congress.'

John Ogle/Oxfam

FORTY YEARS OF DEVELOPMENT

India at Independence was a desperately poor country. Life expectancy stood at only 27.4 years, while numerous contagious diseases, high infant mortality, famines, literacy of 15 per cent and virtually no industry, stood as obstacles to development. Forty years later India's achievement of what are, in official circles, regarded as 'development goods' has been spectacular.

In the years before Independence Nehru and Gandhi stood for two opposing models of development; for Gandhi development had to be centred in the villages: 'The first concern of every village will be to grow its own food, crops and cloth'. For Nehru development meant industrial growth: 'The real test of strength is how much steel you produce, how much power you produce and use'.

With Nehru as Prime Minister, India set out to achieve strength and self-reliance through a 'power and steel-led' industrial strategy. Each of India's Five Year Plans (documents produced by the India Planning Commission which outline the development strategy for the following five years) has pursued this strategy and diverted enormous resources, financial, human and natural, to realise it. In terms of the sights it set for itself, India's development has been highly successful.

India now has the twelfth largest Gross Domestic Product (a measure of all the goods and services that the country produces) in the world, and a skilled labour force second only in size to those of the USSR and US. It has the capacity to manufacture almost anything from lager to tanks to microwave ovens. In 1980, 17 times as much power was generated as in 1951. In 1947 only half of one per cent of villages were electrified; by 1986, 66 per cent had an electricity supply. In 1968 there were only 7,131 banks serving the whole country; by 1985 this had grown to over 52,000, including 30,000 in villages. The railways carry almost 4 billion passengers a year; the postal service is one of the largest in the world, while the press churns out 21,000 dailies and periodicals in all the national languages. It is now estimated that half of India's population is reached by television, while the demand for new sets has reached 2 million a year.

Industrialisation has always been seen as the exciting end of development, yet the fact is that agriculture occupies most workers and supports most of the population. One of the major success stories of India's development has been its ability to feed itself. Foodgrain production (rice, wheat, pulses and so on) has risen by 240 per cent since Independence, while the population has risen by 140 per cent. Buffer stocks of about 20 million tons of grains have been built up, which means that widespread famine is a thing of the past. Indeed, during the African famine of 1985-6 India was the biggest donor of grain, after the US.

For India's 150 million urban middle-class people times have never been so good, the shops so full and medical care and education so readily available.

Why then were there still some 300 million people living in absolute poverty in 1985, according to the Government's own estimates? Why, despite so much impressive growth, is India still among the 22 poorest countries, with the largest number of rural poor people in the world?

A growing body of opinion argues that, after 40 years of development, India will have to take Gandhi's ideas seriously again.

'The economic constitution of India ... should be such that no one should suffer from want of food and clothing ... Everybody should get work ... the elementary necessaries of life ... should be freely available to all as God's air and water are ...'

Mahatma Gandhi

Thermal power station, West Bengal. Since Independence, India has pursued a development policy based on industrialisation, but this policy has been of questionable benefit to the large numbers of rural poor.

ISLANDS OF AFFLUENCE: THE INDIAN ECONOMY

The poverty of the many and the riches of the few are largely a result of India's policy of allowing industrial growth to fuel development. There is a growing gap between the rich and the poor; although the country as a whole is getting richer, the wealth is going to the small number of people who are employed in industry and services. The contribution of agriculture to India's GNP is getting proportionally smaller, but the number of people who earn their living from farming is not. This means that a large proportion of the population is seeing either little change in or a lowering of their incomes.

In the first three decades after Independence India's economy grew slowly (2.5 per cent per annum). Between 1981 and 1989 the growth rate in GDP surged to 5.5 per cent p.a. because changes, such as a reduction in bureaucratic checks, controls, and licensing procedures freed up the economy in a process known as liberalisation. With the boom that followed, India has found itself labelled as one of the Newly Industrialising Countries (NICs), along with Brazil and Mexico. The 'sleeping giant' has woken up and shown some of its enormous potential.

With a growth rate of 8.3 per cent p.a. the manufacturing component of the Indian economy has never been so buoyant. 'Sunrise' industries, such as petrochemicals, synthetic fibres, telecommunications and electronics, are being established at a rapid pace. India is now capable of manufacturing virtually any product, though because little money is put into research and development, new developments rely on foreign collaboration or the outright purchase of technology. Recently, for example, India bought up the factory equipment for constructing the Rover 2000. Sleek new Rovers, known as Standards, are now appearing on crowded city streets.

Not everyone is happy about the new trends in the economy. As L.C. Jain, a member of the Planning Commission, has commented, 'Liberalisation was meant for a few. For the vast majority, it has spelt nothing but disaster.' Others put it differently; Acharya Ramamurthy, a well-known Gandhian, says that 'although our country is free, our villages... are but colonies of economic policy'.

What do they mean by this? There is ample evidence to show that agricultural wages have not risen in real terms since the 1950s. Despite land reform and a 'green revolution', in 1954-5 agricultural workers took home a daily wage of Rs5.75; in 1980-81 they took home Rs5.40 (adjusted to 1979/80 prices). *India Today* comments on the government's 'obsession with industry', and it seems that this obsession prevents any effective attempts to increase the basic agricultural wage. The Economic Survey showed that the output of things like cars, fridges and scooters increased by 19.5 per cent in 1986-87. The growth in rice production for the same period was minimal.

The current industrial boom creates islands of affluence; current economic policy is geared to producing an upper crust of the affluent whose purchasing power, savings and investments will keep the system going. Certainly this sector of the population is growing. In 1980 the country's investor population was two million. By 1989 ten million Indians had invested in the stock-market. Yet for growth to touch the lives of the 70 per cent who depend on agriculture for a living, it must be agriculture and the bounty of the rural environment that changes, not the number of car models available.

Landlord supervising labourers in his fields, in a village near Hyderabad.

Street scene, Hyderabad – a traditional, rural way of life, little changed for centuries, co-exists with a modern, sophisticated industrial society.

'GRASS WITHOUT ROOTS': PLANNING TO END POVERTY

There was nothing cynical in Nehru's concept of centrally planned economic development. In the 1950s it was believed that if the government was strong and industry profitable, the benefits of economic growth would 'trickle down' to the poor. Indian governments have been acutely aware of poverty, but for the first two decades after Independence it was believed that indirect measures (such as employment generation through agriculture or industrial development) were the best way of tackling poverty. By 1969, however, it was clear that the number of poor people was growing, and that these indirect measures were simply making the rich richer.

The Fifth Five Year Plan (1974-1979) was launched by the Congress Party who came to power brandishing the slogan '*Garibi Hatao*' – Banish Poverty. While the overall emphasis of the plan was still to improve the rate of economic growth, a National Minimum Needs Programme was introduced. Minimum needs were defined as elementary education, a drinking water supply, health and nutrition, roads, house sites, electricity, and slum improvement. The aims of the Programme were impressive, but its implementation less effective. Only a third of the money allocated to it was spent.

Successive governments have introduced a variety of schemes aimed at reducing poverty, such as the Integrated Rural Development Programme (IRDP), which provides assets intended to help alleviate poverty such as a cow, sewing machine, or bullock cart, and the Food for Work Programme (FWP). Few countries of the world have shown India's persistence in its attempts to tackle poverty by targeting certain groups. Between 1985 and 1990, Rs10,000 *crore* (£2.9 billion) was allocated to anti-poverty programmes. No nation in the whole of human history has so determinedly attempted positive discrimination to poor individuals.

Despite this, poverty seems to remain little changed. A review of government schemes in the Sixth Five Year Plan is remarkably clear-sighted about the problems:

'The size of the problem which these programmes, especially the individual beneficiary-oriented programmes like...IRDP, have to deal with is enormous. The pace and the manner in which the problem of rural poverty has been dealt with so far leaves much to be desired both qualitatively and quantitatively. Only a small fraction of the rural poor have so far been covered effectively...Even amongst those covered, a sizeable portion is of those who had some land...the landless and rural artisans, who are the poorest, have in most cases been left untouched.'

Many would argue you cannot 'plan' to remove poverty in a country as large and diverse as India, unless you bring into play the resources, energy and ideas of poor people themselves; in fact, to remove poverty altogether would need changes in the structure of society itself. Anti-poverty programmes imply that poverty is a personal problem which can be solved by giving that person a cow, or a sewing machine, regardless of what they themselves think they need. If the people who are being planned for are left out of the planning process, development will fail. Even if centrally planned schemes were implemented perfectly they would at best be a 'bandaid' solution to the problems of poverty – or as L.C.Jain has remarked, 'grass without roots'.

Children, Andhra Pradesh. For poor people, children, far from being a burden, are an asset and an insurance for the future.

AID, DEBT AND GOVERNMENT EXPENDITURE

A redundant tank in a Hyderabad park has become popular with local children.

In the early years of independent India, a cautious policy of self-reliance and the encouragement of domestic savings and investments kept the need for foreign borrowings low. Consequently, India has so far avoided the kind of catastrophic debt crisis that has afflicted some other developing countries.

In the last decade, however, India's borrowing has increased, due partly to the strong emphasis on industrial growth. In terms of billions of dollars, India is now the third biggest Third World debtor, after Brazil and Mexico. Most of India's outstanding loans are to multi-lateral institutions, at concessional rates, but an increasing proportion is to commercial sources, loans which are far more expensive.

In April 1989 India's external debt was officially $42 billion (20 per cent of GNP) and rising, but the long-term debt service ratio of about 24 per cent is much more manageable than that of many African and Latin American countries. However, a confidential 1990 report from the Washington-based Institute of International Finance, quoted in the Indian press, claimed that India's total external debt at the end of March 1989 was over $60 billion, and that the debt service ratio had risen to 38 per cent. If this is the case, India may well be nearing a debt trap.

In 1981 India went to the International Monetary Fund for a loan to tide it over its balance of payments crisis following the oil shock; in 1991 India has again approached the IMF for a loan, to help to meet rising oil costs over the period of the Gulf crisis. The crisis forced thousands of Indians working in the Gulf to return to India, leading to a considerable drop in foreign exchange being repatriated to India. Servicing debts is eating away India's hard-earned foreign exchange, and since imports, which also have to be paid for in other currencies, are rising considerably faster then exports, keeping sufficient reserves of foreign exchange in the country is becoming a problem. Curbing its debts and encouraging saving to support domestic investment is one of the major challenges of the next decade. Unless it does so, India's rate of growth could slow down in the 1990s. This would erode many of the potential gains that a decade of growth has won for India, and could leave many millions of people in India still poor in the year 2000.

India has been receiving about $2 billion annually in official development assistance. The British Overseas Development Administration spends more of its budget on India than any other country; £143.5 million in 1986, or 20 per cent of the entire British bilateral aid programme. (In 1987 a low take-up by the Indian Government reduced this figure to £78.4 million.) But total aid to India amounted to only $2.6 per capita in 1988 (World Bank figures). Papua New Guinea, in contrast, receives the equivalent of $101.9 per capita, and Botswana $127.7, though the net amount of aid they receive is considerably smaller. In this sense, India has been penalised for its size, and the number of its rural poor. The aid it receives is not in proportion to its number of poor people. With the flow of aid diverted towards Sub-Saharan Africa, and debt relief measures targeted towards Latin America, finding the money to invest for the development plans of the next five years will be a major challenge.

It is a little known fact that India itself gives aid to other countries. As of March 1986, some Rs15,100 million (£431.4 million) had been spent on overseas aid, of which 39 per cent was given as loans and 61 per cent as grants. Bhutan received nearly 38 per cent of this Indian foreign aid, Nepal 26.6 per cent and Bangladesh 17.8 per cent, and 15 other countries shared the remainder. India is also a partner in development and economic projects in many countries, and Indian universities and colleges attract students from all over the world, particularly from African countries and the Middle East.

HOW CENTRAL GOVERNMENT SPENT ITS BUDGET IN 1988

Defence:	19.3%
Education:	2.9%
Health:	1.8%
Housing, amenities, social security and welfare:	5.4%
Economic services (expenditure associated with the regulation, support and more efficient operation of business, economic development, redress of regional imbalances, etc.):	21.7%
Other:	49.0%
Total Government expenditure as % of GNP: (UK 37.6%)	17.8%

Source:
IMF Government Finance Statistics Yearbook, 1989, reproduced in World Development Report, 1990, OUP.

A POPULATION EXPLOSION: WHOSE PERSPECTIVE?

India was the first country in the world to have a national family planning programme, established in 1952. By 1985-6, India was spending a massive Rs.651 crore (£186 million) annually on a remarkable system of family planning designed to check the growth of a nation already larger than the combined populations of USA, USSR, Japan and the UK. The Indian family planning system works on the basis of targets; each March the Union Health Ministry sets a target number of 'accepters' (invariably of sterilisation) for individual states. The targets are filtered down to some 15,000 primary health centres, and 98,987 subcentres, with their vast armies of auxiliary nurse midwives, women health visitors and village health guides (some 513,000 individuals). It is their job to make sure that the state meets its target.

By 1988 official statistics claimed that somewhere around 44 million couples in India were 'protected' against pregnancy, very largely through sterilisation. The percentage of married women using contraception (including sterilisation) is estimated to be 35 per cent. Despite this, population growth in India has not changed significantly for a decade. Each woman still has an average of four or five children (1988 total fertility rate: 4.2; UK total fertility rate: 1.8). A baby is born every 1.2 seconds adding 70,000 new babies a day. The total population of India grows by some 16 million a year – the size of Australia. One of the problems of basing a family planning system on sterilisation is that women and men will only have the operation once they feel they've already had enough children – which in India may be four or five.

Many people believe that India has a serious population problem. The growing middle-classes, those who have benefited so much from the development of the past four decades, are deeply worried by the threat to the stability of India's economy that such vast numbers represent. An article in the influential *India Today* argued in 1988 that 'the country's rapidly multiplying numbers is the single biggest factor inhibiting speedier development'. This perspective has been countered by another: The Centre for Science and the Environment maintains that, properly managed, India's fertile lands could support a population two and a half times larger than the billion projected for the year 2000.

Leela's story

'I had eight children; one little boy died when he was just one. I was pregnant again, and had no milk to feed him with. He just got too weak. My eldest daughter died soon after she was married. She committed suicide. She was unhappily married. Why did I have eight children? My husband wanted them. He wanted lots of children to make him wealthy, but now times have changed. We live in a city, and you have to pay for everything. School fees, medicines, clothes, food, fuel for cooking, everything costs money. Now my next daughter is expecting. I have told her, only have two. Any more is crazy.'

Mother and child session at a rural clinic. If women feel that their children have a good chance of surviving into adulthood, they are more likely to want to have smaller families.

Rural children share the tasks of caring for livestock from a very early age and their labour is an important element in the family economy.

Interpreting India's population growth rather depends on which perspective you adopt. Population growth is not often perceived as a threat by the majority of India's rural poor, those who have been virtually by-passed in the development of the last 40 years. Children are not seen as an epidemic to be curbed. As Rafael Salas of the UN Fund for Population Activities has argued, 'large families in the Third world are an intelligent response to people's economic circumstances'.

The idea of children as an economic liability is essentially middle-class. For poor people, children are an asset. By the time they are seven or eight they can contribute to family life by collecting firewood, tending animals and watching younger children, which frees adult members of the family to earn money outside the house. High infant mortality (between 1 in 8 and 1 in 10 babies die in their first year in India) means that women have more children to ensure that some survive into adulthood. It has been calculated that an Indian couple must have an average of 6.3 children in order to have a 95 per cent certainty that just one son will survive until the father is 65 years old. In a country where there is no welfare state, parents depend on their sons to provide for them when they are no longer able to support themselves.

A careful look at the lives of poor Indian women shows that women do in fact limit their family size. The average number of surviving children in Indian families is just over four, far below the potential number of children a family could have. A recent study showed that the average birth interval between children is three years, and many women have no more children after their mid-thirties. Abstinence, prolonged breast feeding, and village-level abortions prevent far more births than India's family planning programme.

Family planning programmes rarely work when they attempt to control women's reproduction while leaving every other aspect of their lives unchanged. A number of studies have shown that when girls are given a primary education and live in circumstances where their children are less likely to fall ill and die, and when they are given a choice of family planning methods, the birth rate always begins to fall.

Consequently, the birth rate among India's urban middle classes is already falling rapidly. Perhaps India cannot afford to wait for a general increase in the standard of living to bring down the birth rate. It seems that the population issue needs to be tackled on two fronts. India's poor rural people need better health care, education and a more certain income, but this needs to go hand in hand with a family planning service which is sensitive to the needs of village women, offers a wider choice of methods, proper care, and follow-up.

Laxmi's story

'In my village a number of women had already gone for the operation. Some experienced pain afterwards and couldn't work as well, but most stayed strong. Moni, my second son gave me a hard time while he was being born. Now I had two sons I thought that we would manage with them. I gave birth in my mother's house. When the time came to return to the village I told my mother that I was returning to my husband, and my husband thought I was with my mother. Taking Moni, I went to the hospital 8 kms away and had the operation. It was difficult being alone and trying to cope with the baby, and my stomach hurt terribly afterwards. Later when I told my husband, he beat me badly. I knew he would never have let me go if I'd asked him. I got Rs200 after the operation, and I certainly don't regret having had it done.'

ENVIRONMENT: A CRISIS IN THE MAKING?

Many Indians argue that the most vital issue facing India is not population, but the condition of its environment. The majority of Indians live in close contact with the natural world. Their needs are met directly from the countryside, rather than from shops. Food comes from the land; fuel, fodder, building materials and fruits from local trees; manure for their fields from animals and leaves, and the raw materials for crafts and rural industry from all sorts of different plants. Anil Argawal, who founded the influential Centre for Science and Environment, writes, 'The environment is not just pretty trees and tigers, threatened plants and ecosystems. It is literally the entity on which we all subsist.'

The purity of rivers, the depth of ground water, the density of forests and the fertility of the soil are taking on a new significance. If India is to feed a population of over a billion in the next century the task of protecting these natural assets and safeguarding their use for village people is both urgent and essential. Village people depend on the land in a way which is not easy to appreciate in the industrialised West. Once land is eroded, or a river polluted, the people who rely on the land for farming, or the river for fishing, are no longer able to earn a living; there may be very little alternative employment.

There is no shortage of government policies to protect the environment, but despite many departments with responsibility for wastelands, water, irrigation, agriculture and forestry, coordination is weak and policies are not rigorously pursued. Powerful industrial lobbies often backed with international finance contribute to environmental destruction as they pursue the raw materials needed for modern industry. Dams and mining have destroyed vast tracts of land, including the traditional homelands of tribal people; industrial pollution, with Bhopal as its most potent symbol, threatens the quality of life in cities and the countryside. It has been estimated that nearly half the industrial output of India uses natural

materials – cotton textiles, rayon, paper, plywood, rubber, soap, sugar, tobacco, jute, chocolate, food processing and packaging, and many more. As these industries expand, they make demands on more land, often replacing food production with cash crops. The waste products created in the process add pollution to the equation.

One of the most important developments of the last decade has been the growth of a strong environmental movement in India, although many would argue that India's villagers, particularly women, have always lived in harmony with their surroundings. The Chipko movement, in which village women embraced the trees of their local forests to prevent them from being cut down, is a recent example of a sensitivity to the natural world which characterises village life. The movement to save India's environment has articulate representatives and excellent documentation, which means that the case for the environment is hard to ignore.

In the next few pages we look at some of the key environmental issues facing India, from the struggle to keep common lands accessible to village people, to the pressures on forests, coastal areas, water sources and agriculture. In each case the ecological balance that has existed for centuries between people and natural resources has come under threat. And in each area strong movements on behalf of the environment and the people who depend on it have begun to emerge.

'India can have a very rich and green future with milk and honey for everyone. India can become a vast desert. It is for Indians to choose.'
Centre for Science and Environment

Air pollution is an increasing problem in India, as in most other industrialised countries.

COMMON LANDS AND WASTELANDS

Some estimates suggest that almost half of India's land is already suffering from serious problems such as the erosion of top soil. Recently, much debate in India has focused on the 'common lands', often referred to as wastelands. The category of wasteland was a British invention. It had little to do with the growing capacity of a piece of land, but more to do with the amount of tax that could be collected from it. Uncultivated land was 'lost' to the revenue collector and was known as wasteland. Under British rule, much of this uncultivated common land, traditionally used communally by all the members of a village, was taken over by the government. Many forest areas, for example, that had been held in common were now 'reserved' for and managed by the government.

Almost one third of India's population have little or no land of their own, and these so-called wastelands make a big difference to their livelihood. They are the lands to which even the poorest people have access; they are used for grazing animals, for collecting twigs, leaves, herbal medicines and the raw materials for village crafts. One study of 21 districts in 7 different states estimated that the income derived by families from common lands was as high as Rs530-830 a year. This land used to belong to villages themselves, but nowadays much of it is government-owned.

Vital though these stretches of common land are, most of them are faced with serious problems. Many of them are indeed slowly turning into wastelands. Pressure on these lands comes partly from India's large number of domestic animals and partly from neglect; villagers no longer think of their commons as their own to take care of. More recently, policies aimed at irrigating commonlands for agriculture or using them for planting trees, which do not supply poor people with firewood or fodder for their animals, has made the problem worse.

Yet, according to the Centre for Science and Environment, this is a problem with a solution. It has been estimated that India's grasslands – many of which are common lands – could produce between five and ten times more fodder for hungry animals. With careful management, the existing croplands could produce more than enough to feed India's growing population, so that further encroachment on common lands for growing food would become unnecessary.

Experiments in some villages, where the villagers themselves have got together and planned the regeneration of the whole village eco-system, have produced spectacular results. India's ecology is such that, left to itself, land rapidly returns to forest; trees and shrubs readily take root and grow. The village of Sukhomajri near Chandigarh, for example, was suffering from badly degraded forest land in the catchment area of its irrigation tank. By protecting the forest area the villagers have increased the amount of water available for their crops, and the quantity of grass and fodder for their animals. Crop production has increased nearly threefold, and the village animals are now giving much more milk. Annual household incomes have risen in just five years by an estimated Rs2000-3,000.

It is argued that such successful regeneration can best be brought about by village people themselves, but only when the common lands are under their own control.

Billboard put up by the Forest Department, as part of a campaign to raise environmental awareness.
John Ogle/Oxfam

THE FORESTS

'What do the forests bear?
Soil, water and pure air.
Soil, water and pure air
Sustain the earth and all she bears.'
   Chorus sung by women in the Chipko movement

'Give me an oak forest and I will give you pots full
of milk and baskets full of grain.'
   Sung by hill women.

Forests are the lungs and reservoirs of India as well as the traditional home of some 54 million tribal people. Of the 7,000 plant and animal species found only in India, most live in the forests. The forests of the Western Ghats, for example, the chain of mountains that run 1,600 kilometres down the western side of India, are the source of forty major rivers and innumerable streams; these forests regulate the water cycle and most of the ecological processes of Peninsular India.

Yet India's natural forests are dying. While national forest policy maintains that at least one third of the country should be under good forest cover to keep the ecological balance of the country stable, today only about 10 per cent of India remains densely wooded. Every year another 1.5 million hectares of forests are felled, bulldozed and burnt. Only forty years ago India's wooded lands were still the forests of Kipling's *Jungle Book*, full of wild animals. If deforestation continues at the current rate, India could enter the twenty-first century with no original forests left at all.

Trees keep the ecological cycle stable. Roots hold the soil in place and rotting leaves replace humus. When trees are felled and the land is not replanted there is little to check the erosion of the top soil. Heavy monsoon rains wash irreplaceable top soil into reservoirs, rivers and the sea in such quantities that it is estimated that India loses as much top soil every six months as has been used to build all the brick houses in the country.

Eroded land can be used for little else; and inevitably it is poor people who suffer the consequences of damaged land and disappearing forests. One study estimated that women in some areas spend up to nine hours a day simply looking for the wood to cook their meals.

Why are forests being felled? There are several factors at work. One is the increasing demands of industry. Trees are the main source of pulp for paper, rayon and other cellulose products. Forests provide poles for construction, sleepers for railways and hardwood for furniture. Another factor is the demand for fuel wood. Around 75 per cent of wood felled each year is burnt for fuel, domestic and industrial. Mining, dams and plantations take their toll of forests. Village people are often forced by poverty into cutting wood to sell. A study of a woodlot in an area of Karnataka found that 12 per cent of the trees were being cut down each year, but that 78 per cent went for fuel wood to Bangalore.

In response to the urgent need for more trees the government launched one of the most ambitious reforestation programmes in the world. Five million hectares were to be planted with trees every year; foreign funds were mobilised to carry out a programme that was known as 'social forestry', because of its objective of supplying the fodder and fuel needs of poor people. Huge plantations of eucalyptus and casuarina have sprung up, and recent reports show that India's forest cover is at last beginning to increase. The success with which social forestry has met its other objectives, however, is a more mixed story.

SOCIAL FORESTRY IN KARNATAKA

Karnataka has a large social forestry programme. The programme is of particular interest because 40 per cent of its funding came from the British ODA (the remaining 48 per cent comes from the World Bank and 12 per cent from Indian sources). The Karnataka programme has three components: farm forestry, which encourages farmers to grow trees on private land by providing them with free seedlings; nurseries which enable families to raise saplings by giving them seeds and plastic bags, and thirdly, tree planting on government-owned village common lands for fuel and animal fodder.

How successful has social forestry been? By 1985 it was becoming clear that the main beneficiaries of social forestry were the large farmers who were planting eucalyptus as a cash crop for sale to pulpwood industries, on land which had previously grown food crops. Many had received thousands of free seedlings. An unfortunate consequence of tree farming has in some cases been to reduce the number of jobs available, since tree growing employs fewer people than growing food crops on the same area. Women have lost out more than men, since men tend to be employed for digging, felling and other heavy work. Poorer farmers with smaller farms are unable to wait seven to ten years for the return on their investments, so are much less willing to plant trees.

The planting of village common lands which had been transferred to the forestry department was intended to be of most benefit to poor people. Unfortunately, when the plantations were first developed they too were almost always planted with eucalyptus. While eucalyptus may be useful commercially, it is useless as a fodder crop since animals won't eat it. These common land plantations seems in fact to have served industry's needs for raw materials, rather than the needs of poor people. Villagers were rarely consulted about the placing of plantations or the type of trees planted. Most villagers were unaware that the trees were intended to benefit them, and had little interest in protecting them.

Well-organised and well-publicised campaigning from local organisations in Karnataka and lobbying in the UK is slowly changing the pattern of social forestry in Karnataka. Eucalyptus is no longer the only tree planted, but trees for fruit, fodder and fuel are appearing on common lands.

Planting trees can bring poor people many benefits. With even a few trees a family can have an adequate supply of fuel, fruit, green leaf manure and timber. A number of voluntary organisations are exploring ways of working with the forestry department which will put the needs of poor people first, and make tree growing effective and the eventual greening of India a real possibility.

'...Here, exploitation takes the form of planting an eucalyptus forest on land previously available for villagers. Cattle and sheep could be grazed there; local craftsmen could gather the grass and vines needed to weave baskets and mats; women could gather branches and leaves for cooking fuel; seasonal fruits and herbs could be picked free.

Since the area was planted with eucalyptus saplings, the poorest villagers have been the hardest hit. Nothing else grows where eucalyptus is planted; no grass, no undergrowth, no flowers; no animal will touch its bark or leaves. No birds sing, for no bird will nest there...'

Ajit Bhattacharjea, Deccan Herald, 19 November, 1987.

PEOPLE OF THE FORESTS

India's forests are the home of the *adivasis*, which means the 'original people' of India. Long before India was invaded by the Aryans, tribal people lived in the forests, hunting animals and gathering plants, roots and fruit for food. Some tribal groups cleared patches of the jungle to plant gardens. When the land became less fertile they moved on and allowed the jungle to reclaim the land. With a real stake in making sure the forests survived, tribal groups developed a number of traditions to protect it. Certain areas were considered sacred, and trees such as the mango, peepul, tamarind and banyan were never felled.

There are at least 400 tribal groups left in India – 7.5 per cent of India's population – each with its own language and customs. Despite the enormous changes that began during British rule, most tribal people keep their distinctive cultures. They live mainly in central and eastern India, in particular Madhya Pradesh, Orissa, Arunachal Pradesh, the Himalayan Frontier and the forested areas of the south, though smaller tribal communities are found all over India.

Today, however, relatively few tribal people remain undisturbed in the forests. Many have lost their traditional lands, and in the process have become some of the poorest and most vulnerable members of Indian society.

Why have tribal people lost their lands? The traditional homelands of tribal people are the sites of abundant natural resources – timber, minerals and water. As India has modernised, the need for more minerals, water and wood has led to a conflict of interests between tribal people and modern industry. Generally, tribal people have been the losers, and deforestation, mining and the construction of large dams have been enormously disruptive to their traditional way of life. By the Government's own estimates, 8.5 million tribal people have been displaced by large-scale development projects since Independence and of these, very few indeed have been properly compensated and resettled.

As we have seen, legislation established by the British transferred ownership of the forests to the State, rather than to the people who lived in them. More recent legislation, designed to protect the forests, has left forest-dwelling tribal people only minimal rights to collect fruit, wood and grass, either for their own use, or for sale. Instead, tribal livelihoods are increasingly tied up with the forestry departments and contractors, for whom they work on a daily basis. The construction of some 300 wild-life sanctuaries, to conserve forests and to encourage tourism, has resulted in large numbers of tribal families being moved on. Many of them now work in the sanctuaries.

Tribal people living in areas with great mineral wealth have suffered a similar fate. The tribal area in southern Bihar, for example, is one of the richest mining areas in India with more than 25 per cent of the country's total mining carried out there. Many tribal people have had their lands taken over for mining, and their worship and burial grounds destroyed in the process. These original owners are forced to work as coolies on their own lands.

The building of dams can have serious consequences for tribal communities. In the worst case, their homelands are flooded, as for example when the Rihard Dam in Singrauli, Madhya Pradesh was built. The dams planned in the Narmada Valley Development Project could submerge an estimated 350,000 hectares of forest, threatening the livelihood of over a million people, many of them tribals.

The plight of tribal people in India raises important questions. The juggernaut of 'development' demands huge quantities of natural resources, but these resources have high human and environmental costs. Many Indian writers and activists are questioning the type of development that destroys the environment and the life-styles of indigenous people. Tribal people themselves are coming together and organising their own resistance and protest, against large dams and the loss of their lands and are working to revive their religious and cultural traditions. Out of this has come the Jharkhand Movement, in which tribals from Bihar, Orissa, West Bengal and Madhya Pradesh are demanding the formation of their own tribal state, Jharkhand.

If you don't have an umbrella, a large leaf will do quite well instead! Wet day in the Dangs.

These hand-made wicker 'umbrellas' are often seen in the forests of the Dangs, a region of extremely high rainfall.

IN THE FORESTS OF THE DANGS

When the British set up their first trading station in Surat in 1612 they had their eye on the fine teak forests of the Dangs as a source of wood for their navy. The Dangs is a small district in the south of Gujarat and is the home of two tribal groups, the Kokanis and the Bhils. To get into the Dangs from the north you have to cross the Ambika River, gateway to one of the few areas of India still under thick forest. Teak and bamboo plantations intersperse with natural jungle on gently undulating hills, and in the rainy season the overwhelming greenness of the district is a reminder of the richness of India's original forests.

Living in the Dangs is not always easy. Health services, education and communications are poor and the forest is closely guarded by forest officials. In the past ten years the Gram Vikas Mandali Association Trust (GVMAT) has been working in the area. In the village of Borigartha, GVMAT helped the villagers to set up an irrigation cooperative which after three years of hard work has managed to get a grant of Rs5 *lakhs* (£14,000) from the government. This will cover the cost of lifting water from the Kapri river to irrigate about 40 hectares of village land. GVMAT also helps villagers to set up village groups, called *mandals*, to work for the changes they want in their village. The *mandal* in Borigartha has recently opened a village shop – the only one in the village – while in nearby Hanwatchand the village *mandal* set up a flour mill, saving considerable time for the women who previously ground all their wheat and millet by hand.

Giradaledar is another village where GVMAT has started working, invited by the women of the village who had seen the developments in Borigartha. Saruben, who works for GVMAT and helped set up the women's group, commented on the changes taking place: 'When we first started the meetings none of the women spoke or participated. Now they've lost a lot of their shyness. Having talked about their problems, for example, the lack of a dispensary, they feel they can do something about it.' So the village women recently wrote to the State government requesting a dispensary. Soniben, a woman from Giradaledar explained, 'They could hardly believe they'd got such a letter from a group of village women, and they sent someone to find out what was going on! We still don't have a proper dispensary, but they've given us a supply of medicines for malaria and other infections. It's a good start.'

The people of Giradaledar have also challenged the forest officials over access to the jungle. Villagers are allowed to take wood from the forest to build their own houses but claiming this right can sometimes lead to confrontation with forest guards. Soniben recently made local history when she stood up to the guards. She asked them, 'Why are you treating us like this? We aren't tigers. We are people like you. This wood is brought for building a house, which everyone needs. Don't you have houses to stay in? We are *adivasis*, we live in the jungles, protect them from fire, and we have a right to these jungles.'

For people like Soniben, living in the forests of the Dangs is a way of life that her people have followed for centuries. Protecting her right to use it means preserving something of her heritage as a tribal woman. Or as she put it, 'The jungle is all that we know. We live in the jungle and we love the jungle. Yes, there are problems, but just as your home is the city, our home is the jungle.'

Soniben and her friends from Giradaledar.

WATER

India is one of the wettest countries in the world; recently it has also become one of the thirstiest. The paradox of water – the co-existence of floods with droughts, vast irrigation networks with dried-up wells – is another area in which large-scale development projects seem to have worked against the interests of poorer people.

India has traditionally been a nation of water storers; few villages were without specially constructed reservoirs, called tanks, and wells to collect monsoon rainwater. People adapted to the amount of rainfall nature provided them with. The size of India means that different regions have different rainfall patterns. Some parts of India are described as 'water-scarce'; others as 'water abundant'. Yet even in the driest areas of India, such as Rajasthan, intricate networks of tanks, channels and wells ensured that there was always drinking water; indigenous engineering provided irrigation for crops, and only crops that were suitable for the local climate were planted.

Women have always been the water providers for their families and could produce good water to drink even when surface supplies were muddy. In some parts of India a seed of the nirmali tree is rubbed against the inside of clay water pots until the mud coagulates and sinks to the bottom of the pot, taking all other impurities with it.

In some senses, the water shortage in India is a man-made phenomenon. Tanks and channels which were once looked after by village communities have been allowed to fall into disrepair. Private ownership of a water source – a borewell, for example – has undermined these community assets. Access to water for agriculture may now depend on being rich enough to dig a well and buy a pump set. As trees have been cut down in the catchment areas of tanks, soil erosion and tank siltation mean less water is collected. Deforestation also leads to a changing rainfall pattern, and some rivers that once flowed all the year round are now dry except just after the monsoon. Vandana Shiva argues that large-scale water projects have diverted and dammed rivers, so they no longer replenish the underground water downstream, and wells and smaller rivers dry up. In parts of Maharashtra land has recently been irrigated for sugar cane, which has lowered the water table, and left poor farmers who rely on dug wells literally high and dry.

The fact that water has now to be brought by bullock carts into villages identified as having 'no water source' nearby shows the tragic breakdown of village self-sufficiency. How could villages have survived so long if they were really without water sources?

Environmentalists such as Vandana Shiva point out the self-defeating aim of large-scale water projects. She explains that the failure to 'think like a river' and follow the logic of a particular river's flow, means that such projects end up by worsening the problem of water scarcity for all but a minority served directly by the new irrigation systems. Rajiv Gandhi raised some different criticisms: 'the situation today is that since 1951, 246 big surface irrigation projects have been initiated. Only 65 of these have been completed...For 16 years we have poured money out. The people have got nothing back, no irrigation, no water, no help in their daily life...'

Village people are beginning to tackle the problem of water shortages. In the South women and men have started the task of renovating the tanks by desilting them and replanting trees in the catchment areas. In the North, protest movements against large dams, deforestation, and the destruction of the soil, are growing in strength.

A traditional water-seller in Old Delhi.

Lack of access to clean water can be a major problem. Indian women have to do the best they can to provide drinking water for their family, sometimes from muddy sources like this one.

SAVING THE RAIN

Dharmapuri, an area of Tamil Nadu, is a very dry place. In some years, it only rains two or three times. In a good year most poor farmers manage to grow one lot of crops, usually a mixture of maize, millet, lentils, tomatoes and chillies, but in a bad year many families migrate to Bangalore in search of alternative work. There is water, but it is a long way underground; some people have dug wells and still not found any water 40 metres down.

Eleven years ago, a young man called Francis decided that he wanted to work with poor people in Dharmapuri, rather than finish his training and become a priest. He moved into a village and began meetings with local people. Water was their biggest problem; there was no water for cattle to drink and no water for irrigating crops. Francis approached Oxfam, who suggested that he visit another project, already funded by Oxfam in Karnataka where villagers had started building 'check' dams. By now Francis had started a project, the Integrated Village Development Project (IVDP). IVDP decided that check dams might solve the water problem in some of the villages of Dharmapuri, and, with Oxfam funds, constructed the first dam in a village called Panchal Thunai.

A check dam is a very small dam that blocks a stream and creates a tiny reservoir. Its main function is to replenish the ground water in a radius of about 3 kilometres around the dam. In Panchal Thunai the water table rose to within seven metres of the ground; wells that had been dry began to fill up; new wells were sunk, and the reservoir was a source of water for thirsty animals. Since 1983 IVDP have built ten more check dams. Village people construct the dams themselves, which provides them with work and an income. Once the dams are constructed and the water table rises, villagers take interest free loans from IVDP's credit scheme to cover the cost of digging wells to irrigate their land. A system of village committees ensures that all the loans are repaid. The availability of water means that instead of one crop a year, there are now three crops. Three crops a year means agricultural work all the year round so that even families with no land of their own are benefiting from the extra work available. Migration from the villages with check dams has completely stopped.

Water is transforming the parts of Dharmapuri where IVDP works. According to Francis, 'Water is paramount. In a drought-prone area like this, unless you can find water, you can't do anything. Now, even in years where the rains are poor, we can save the little rain that falls and make maximum use of it.'

Carrying water up from a step well. Collecting and transporting water can take up a lot of time and energy.

Check dam built by IVDP.
Keith Mason/Oxfam

FISHING

Over many centuries about 2,400 fishing villages have developed along India's 6,400 kilometres of coastline. Different seas, different fish and different seascapes have led to many fishing styles. On the calm waters off the west coast fishermen use wooden dugouts and other large canoes, while catamarans are more popular on the open, high-surf seas of southern and eastern India. Indian fisherfolk are among the most skilful in the world. A great variety of techniques and gears have been developed to catch different sorts of fish at different times of the year, at the same time protecting eggs, young fish and other marine life.

India's rich seas are matched by the wealth of fresh water fish found in the great river systems, extensive irrigation networks and the standing water of the paddy-fields. The years since Independence have seen a number of attempts to increase the harvest from seas and rivers. The Bay of Bengal Programme, for example, a multilaterally funded project on India's east coast, is developing low-technology boats to enable local fishermen to catch fish safely, further out to sea. The most significant recent development, however, has been the mechanisation of small boats and the introduction of trawlers.

By 1980 there were around 19,000 mechanised boats and something in the region of 135,000 traditional craft catching India's 2 million tonnes of marine fish. Local fishermen mechanise their boats by fixing an outboard motor on the back. The first outboard motors imported into India had been designed for pleasure boats in the West and were useless in Indian conditions. Many fishing families who invested in them have been left in debt. Using an outboard motor brings with it a range of benefits but an equal range of problems. John Kurien, who has worked extensively with fishing communities in Kerala, has pointed out that a fisherman using an outboard motor needs to catch seven times more fish to break even.

One of the ironies about the introduction of more 'effective' ways of catching fish is that the total amount of fish caught is declining. In Kerala, for example, the annual catch between 1971-1975 was around 400,000 tonnes. In 1987 it was only 287,000 tonnes. Local fishermen blame the trawlers that sweep the sea bed clean, killing off eggs and young fish.

Fisherwomen are generally responsible for local, small-scale marketing of fish. With the introduction of trawling, women face competition from fish-merchants who can afford to buy up the whole catch. A large proportion of the catch in Maharashtra and Kerala is going to big dealers with ice trucks, often for export.

Fishermen on inland waters are not faring much better, but here the problems are to do with pollution and the creation of dams which block the flow of rivers. Almost all Indian rivers are polluted. Untreated sewage, industrial waste, and run-off from fertilisers and pesticides, are threatening many stretches of water and the livelihood of those who fish on them. India's fishing communities have good organisations – such as the National Fishermen's Forum – who are determined to focus attention on the problems of fishing communities.

Most of the small-scale, local marketing of fish is carried out by women. Here, they wait on the beach for the catch to be landed.
John Ogle/Oxfam

There are a great variety of traditional fishing craft and styles of fishing around India's coasts. Fishermen who use small boats like this are finding it harder to make a living, as over-fishing by large trawlers is reducing fish-stocks.
Pete Davis/Oxfam

FISHING FOR A LIVING

Theresa makes her living selling fish. She stood and watched the fragile looking catamaran bounce on the waves. When the boat came in, and the basket of bright silver fish had been tipped on to the beach, Theresa along with five other fisher women, began bidding for the catch. Theresa's bid of Rs70 was the highest, and she put the catch – about seven kilos, she estimated – in an aluminium pot which her friend helped her lift on to her head. 'This fish isn't very popular,' she explained, 'Which is why it is so cheap. I'll take the train from here to Trivandrum, and sell it in the market, but I'll have to be quick!' She walked off swiftly down the beach.

In Kerala, women from fishing communities do most of the local marketing of fish. Finding the capital to buy fish from the beach when the catch comes in is a perennial problem. Women usually go to local money lenders but are charged high interest. If a woman borrows Rs100, the money lender will only give her Rs90, the extra Rs10 being charged as interest for the day. Repaying the Rs100 may mean that a woman loses half her day's profits to the money lender. This problem of working capital has been solved for many fishing communities by the Trivandrum District Fishing Federation. Among the many activities TDFF has helped to set up, women's credit unions have been among the most popular. Soosamma is the secretary of the Fishing Co-operative Society in a village called Fatimapura. She took a loan from the credit union of her village, for which Oxfam provided the working capital. 'I've used the money to pay off old debts,' she said, 'and for my marketing work. I pay it back just a little at a time – one day Rs5, and another day Rs2.'

Gracie and Selestina, now in their mid-forties, were class mates at school. Now they work on the beach together as saleswomen, in a village called Anjeglo. As the fish are auctioned, Gracie and Selestina write down details of each transaction. No money changes hands on the beach, but instead, the fishermen are given a chit which they can cash later in the Fishing Society office in the village. When the market women return in the evening from selling their fish, Gracie and Selestina collect money from them for the fish they bought in the morning. In this way, fishing and fish marketing is kept firmly in the hands of local communities, removing the need for middlemen.

Gracie explained, 'I was born here, raised here and married here. All my family have worked in fishing. When I was a younger woman, we faced so many difficulties. Now we still face difficulties, but this work that I do helps many women considerably. Anything to get out of the clutches of the money lenders!'

Soosamma, the secretary of the Fishing Co-operative in Fatimapura village.
Julia Mosse/Oxfam

Theresa setting off to market.
Julia Mosse/Oxfam

AGRICULTURE

Croplands cover 43 per cent of India's land area. The 142 million hectares that grow the cereals, pulses, vegetables, fruit and spices that feed India also provide an income for some 70 million families or 65 per cent of India's population. In North America, the same area of cultivated land supports only 4 million families.

Agriculture has been one of the most visible success stories in India since Independence. In the 1950s and 60s the widening food deficit meant an expensive reliance on imported food grains. Continuous droughts from 1964 to 1967 and the ensuing famine in Bihar that left thousands starving led to emergency imports of grain from the US. International doom-watchers predicted that millions of Indians would die of starvation in the 1970s. Yet the drought in India of 1986-88 which affected all of the main agricultural states and led to a shortfall in food production comparable to that of the Sahelian droughts of the 1980s resulted in neither mass starvation nor mass emigration. Instead, government buffer stocks tided the country over until the successful harvest of the following year. Clearly, in the years since 1967 Indian agriculture had been transformed.

At Independence India produced about 50 million tonnes of food grains a year. By the 1988-89 harvest this had shot up to a record 170 million tonnes a year, a 240 per cent increase. The population has only grown by 140 per cent in the same period.

The green revolution, as this transformation in agriculture is called, occurred towards the end of the 1960s. High-yielding varieties (HYVs) of wheat and rice were developed, and Indian agricultural scientists modified them to suit Indian conditions. A National Seed Corporation and State Farm Corporation were set up in 1966 to produce seed, and thousands of test demonstrations were carried out. Uptake was enormous.

It was a conscious strategy of the green revolution to 'build on the best' and promote the new seeds to farmers who had flat, irrigated lands and fertile soils. For such farmers the changes brought about by these 'miracle' seeds were indeed revolutionary. HYVs require large amounts of fertiliser and controlled amounts of water. Those able to afford the complete package (which included pesticides and herbicides) made big profits. Farmers in the Punjab, Haryana, parts of Tamil Nadu and in other pockets throughout India, benefited the most. In the Punjab, yields rose from under 1 tonne per hectare to 3.3 tonnes.

The majority of India's farmers, however, do not cultivate flat, irrigated croplands. Most of those who live off the land are poor subsistence farmers, growing a living for themselves and their families on land watered by rain water, often in hilly areas and in places where deforestation and erosion have left their mark. They cultivate a variety of different crops and use a technology unchanged for hundreds of years. The green revolution has simply passed them by.

Small vegetable plot, showing many different plants growing together; near Bhubaneswar, Orissa.
Liz Clayton/Oxfam

'It is wonderful, too, how much is known of rotation, the system of 'mixed crops' and of fallowing ... I, at least, have never seen a more perfect picture of cultivation.'

J.A.Voelker,
Report on the Improvement of Indian Agriculture, 1893.

An embankment, running between rice fields. Rice is a major food crop in India, and is transplanted when the land is flooded, after the monsoon rains.

HOW GREEN WAS THE REVOLUTION?

There have been a number of criticisms of the green revolution. The environmental costs of growing single crops intensively are only now being appreciated. High levels of fertilisers can leave poisonous nitrates in the water supply; irrigation on land used only to rain water can cause water-logging where the soil does not drain properly; HYVs rapidly use up the nutrients in the soil; and pesticides used in large quantities poison the farmers who handle them, the food produced, and the rest of the environment. Critics of green revolution farming argue that increased food production using these methods has only been brought about at great cost to the environment.

Green revolution farming has not been without its social costs either. Almost inevitably, the larger farmers became richer and the smaller farmers had to sell off land to repay debts incurred when they bought the green revolution 'package', which is only really cost-effective on large farms. Farmers who previously had tenants on their land have found it more profitable to farm the land themselves and employ seasonal labour, so that many former tenants have found themselves working as landless labourers.

It has also been argued that success in producing large quantities of wheat and rice disguises failures in other respects. The production of pulses, oilseeds and other cereal crops, important contributions to the diet of poor people, has hardly risen since Independence. Critics argue that surpluses have been created only because India's poorest people can't afford to buy all the food they need. One of India's leading nutritionists, Dr. C. Gopalan, suggests that 'our buffer stocks are apparently more an indication of the poverty of our masses than of real food surplus'.

Green revolution farming is only half the story of Indian agriculture. As we have seen, most Indian farmers do not just grow one cereal crop. They use intricate systems of farming which may involve planting up to five different crops in different patterns in the same field. This is to try and get the maximum amount of food from the land, while making sure that if one crop fails there will still be something left. These intercropping systems often lead to healthier crops; the predators of one crop may keep at bay the predators of the others. Intercropping has special benefits for the soil as well, fixing nitrogen and conserving fertility. Manure and humus are regularly returned to the soil, and shallow ploughing by ox-plough helps to keep the land healthy. Over the centuries, Indian cultivators, frequently women, have developed an almost perfect relationship with the land around them.

Nowadays, however, many Indian farmers, particularly those farming in hilly areas, are finding it difficult to make a living from their land. Some of the recent changes in the environment, such as deforestation and soil erosion, are causing problems. Farm sizes are also getting smaller as India's population grows.

A growing population will need more food. Green revolution farming cannot be expanded indefinitely, so the concern in India is to increase the food grown on traditional farms. Farmers themselves are becoming co-researchers and traditional techniques are being linked with new, appropriate technologies. The potential for growing food in India is enormous. Finding the most effective ways of developing that potential is the challenge.

LAND AND LANDLESSNESS

Land means a livelihood. A patch of land, even a small one, means that crops – tomatoes, lentils, chillies – can be grown, either to be eaten or sold. A patch of land can grow trees for fuel, fruit, and green leaf manure. A patch of land is an asset against which a bank will lend you money. Land in rural India is the one thing which decides how well-off you will be.

When a village family has no land they make their living by working on other people's land. The wages of agricultural labourers vary from place to place, but many women can expect to get no more that Rs8 (23p) a day, and men Rs12. Most States have legislation which lays down a minimum wage, but it is seldom enforced. Children from landless families begin contributing to the family income when they are very young, tending the landlord's cattle, for example.

Working as a daily labourer creates many problems. One is the seasonal nature of the work. In the growing season, work may be easy to find but once the harvest is in, agricultural work is scarce. A study carried out in 1984-5 in Bihar, Orissa and Assam found that over a third of landless people could not find work for more than half the year. Two thirds were working for less than seven months a year, and only a tiny minority (4 per cent) were working for more than nine months.

Underemployment matters because there is no welfare state to fall back on. Days without work mean days with little money to buy food or for unexpected events like illness. Migration is one solution. Sometimes families split, as men move away in search of work. At other times the whole family migrates. Tamil families from drought-prone areas migrate to brick kilns outside Madras, building temporary shelters to live in and earning paltry amounts for making bricks. When migration is not part of a traditional life style it can badly disrupt the life of the family.

Landlessness is a relatively recent problem in India. In the past, landless families lived in a close relationship with their landlords. Even when there was little agricultural work, there were other forms of work to be done, often in exchange for food. As these feudal relationships have broken down, landless people have come to rely on earning a daily wage, although they may still be dependent on the good will of local landlords. Since Independence, India has had land reform programmes, and many people have gained rights to tiny plots of land, but often these are not large enough to provide a family income.

Finding solutions to the problems of landlessness takes many forms. Young men often migrate to cities, more or less permanently. Other landless people are beginning to organise themselves to demand higher wages. Cooperatives of landless people can negotiate higher rates for harvesting fields than individuals on their own. In parts of Gujarat and Rajasthan, a revival of traditional handicrafts is providing work in the dry season, and helping to prevent migration.

Basketmaker living on the roadside in Hyderabad. One of a group of tribal forest dwellers who were moved from their homes as part of a scheme to 'protect' the forest.
Liz Clayton/Oxfam

FIELDS OF OUR OWN

'Without my land, I would be an orphan again.' Nirula pointed up the hill towards a landmark of a small mud house. 'To the left of that house, stretching up to the line of trees; that is now my land.' Nirula is a tribal man, living in Gundlupet, in the foothills of the Western Ghats. Three years ago he was working as a labourer in Bandipur, one of India's wild life sanctuaries. In 1973, alarmed at the disappearance of the big cats, India launched 'Project Tiger', to protect wild life from the effects of deforestation and development. Nirula's family was one of the tribal families moved out of its homeland in the depths of the jungle and settled in Bandipur, on the fringes of the forests, where he earned a few rupees a day cutting grass, ditching and making roads.

Six years ago, a young newly-qualified doctor, Dr Maheswara, moved to Gundlupet to work with tribal people. He quickly realised that the issue lying closest to their hearts was not health or education, but land, and the loss of the lands that were their birthright. He started the 'Organisation for Rural Reconstruction', known as DUDE, the word for a tribal drum. DUDE set out to motivate and encourage tribal people to fight back for land of their own. They formed village committees, and put pressure on the Revenue Department to release stretches of land. A couple of years ago Nirula, along with 30 other families, left Bandipur and moved to a hamlet called Channikatte, sharing out 60 hectares between them. Most now have formal land rights, and the others expect to get them soon.

In March 1990 another 50 families left Bandipur and moved to Melakamanahalli, where 48 hectares of land have been allocated to them. Their traditional huts straggle in a line up a low hill. To the left, the newly acquired land stretches out, still covered with shrubs, boulders, and high grass; to the right, the foothills of the Western Ghats. The huts have been built in a line as a barrier to wild elephants, who come down from the forest in search of crops to eat. Bommi, a tribal woman, looked out across the land. 'It is land, it is cultivation, it is a livelihood. If we can cultivate the land we can feed ourselves.' But the land looked inhospitable; hours of back-breaking work lie in front of Bommi and her fellow-villagers before the land becomes the fertile fields of their dreams. 'Come back in two years' time,' said Dr Maheswara, 'and you will see the transformation.'

A visit to the little village of Haggadahalli proves the difference that land makes. Three years ago, the 30 families of the hamlet obtained land rights to some 48 hectares. As we arrived, the evening breeze carried the sound of the village cattle coming home after a day's grazing at the edge of the forest. Rangaiah and Chikamadaya, two of the village elders, sat down to talk about what having land has meant. Chikamadaya explained, 'When DUDE first visited the village, we ran away. We were scared of the "pantwallas". Now, see, we are confident to talk to anyone. Then we had only a quarter of an acre here and there. We organised ourselves into committees, and decided that we would take over the land around. After many battles we succeeded. We grow groundnuts, lentils, sesame seeds and millet. This year the rains failed and we grew very little, so our village committee is starting to look at the possibilities of irrigation. Then we want to tackle the problem of education for the village children.'

In the years since DUDE started work, 550 out of 650 tribal families in Gundlupet have gained land. Not all of them have formal land rights yet, but they are confident that these will come in time. Land is the foundation for everything else; as Nirula said, 'Once we have fields of our own, we are our own people again.'

Villagers, landless and landowners, working together on land reclamation, in West Orissa.
Liz Clayton/Oxfam

ORDERING SOCIETY: THE CASTE SYSTEM

'I go to the village tea-shop, and instead of a glass they give me an old aluminium cup. Well, at least I can go to the tea shop. My father could not. In the school, the plates my children use are marked underneath with a red cross. Well, at least my children can go to the school. My father's children could not. My house is on the edge of the village, and who but my own people will enter and eat with me? My landlord calls me when there is work, and I must go. Escaping from debts I went to the city and got work in a wine shop [in Madras, where partial prohibition is in force]. I did not know that the owner had put the shop in my name. Whenever the police come, it is me they take away. We have to fight for every change, but changes are coming. And we adjust.'

What is caste and where does it come from? The caste system is probably the oldest hierarchical system in the world today with a history stretching back several thousand years. Although there have been plenty of speculations, nobody really knows how the system developed. At some point in the distant past a basic form of the caste system began to emerge. Society was divided into four *varnas* (sanskrit for 'colour'). These *varnas* were the *brahmins* or priests; the *ksatriyas*, or warriors and nobility; the *vaisayas* who were ordinary tribesmen and traders, and the *sudras*, or servant caste. Outside the caste-system altogether were the 'untouchables', who Mahatma Gandhi renamed '*harijans*', meaning 'people of God'.

Over the following centuries, intermarriages between invaders and the people of the subcontinent produced many thousands of castes and subcastes. There are an estimated 40,000 different castes and subcastes in contemporary India. Traditionally each caste had its own hereditary work; children born into a caste of potters would themselves inevitably become potters. Although in cities this hereditary system is breaking down, the son of a village barber is still more likely to be employed as a hairdresser than the son of a washerman.

The division of labour is not the whole story. People usually marry other people from the same caste, and caste groups are ranked in some sort of hierarchy. It is common to hear people refer to themselves as 'high caste' or '*brahmin*'. This hierarchy is based on a religious idea of purity and impurity. This is not a question of cleanliness, but rather an abstract idea to do with closeness or distance to 'polluting' events like death. *Brahmins*, as the purest caste traditionally keep themselves aloof from pollution and are vegetarian, whereas the traditional work of the 'untouchable' communities is tied up with removing pollution: removing dead carcasses and being the village undertakers for example. Separation is all important; *harijan* hamlets often remain separate from the main village, and different caste groups live together in different parts of the settlement.

The caste system has always generated protest. Religious movements and, more recently, political movements have challenged the hierarchical nature of caste and India's constitution abolished untouchability, at least on paper.

Although the hereditary system which links caste with occupation is beginning to break down, it is still likely that the son of a village barber will work as a hairdresser.

Today members of 'scheduled castes' (as over 100 million *harijans* are now called) still face discrimination and oppression. Newspapers periodically carry stories of atrocities committed against *harijans* by members of other castes. The system of 'reservations', which reserves places for *harijans* in central and local government, in public sector industries, the civil service, and throughout the education system, aims to ensure that scheduled caste interests are protected. A recent attempt to extend this system of reservations in 1990 led to widespread s)rotests all over India.

In contemporary India, caste shows no sign of going away, though as an integrated system it is beginning to break down. It nonetheless remains an important factor in the competition for scarce resources - political, economic and educational.

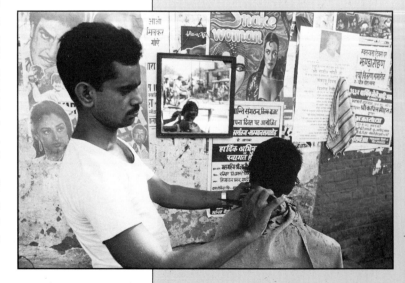

A PLURALITY OF BELIEFS

India's architectural landscape tells the story of the religious diversity of the sub-continent. Mosques and temples, cathedrals and chapels, coexist in the same city alongside sacred trees and wayside shrines. Religions in turn have created a diversity of cultures, and a kaleidoscope of festivals, rituals and celebrations. India is the birth-place of four of the world's religions – Hinduism, Buddhism, Sikhism and Jainism; has embraced Islam and Christianity; offered sanctuary to persecuted Parsis and Jews; and maintained hundreds of ancient nature-worshipping religions. That it has done so suggests a quite extraordinary capacity for variety and tolerance. Moreover, India is a land of active religious practice; atheism and agnosticism have failed to take hold in the way they have in the West.

Of the seven religions practised in India, Hinduism has the largest number of adherents – 82.6 per cent in the 1981 census. Islam is the largest minority; 11.4 per cent of the population are Muslims – well over 75 million people – giving India the fourth largest population of Muslims in the world. Partition altered the ratio of Hindus and Muslims. In 1941 almost a quarter of India's population were Muslims (23.7 per cent), and Hindus only 65.5 per cent. Christians, Sikhs, Buddhists and Jains make up about 5.6 per cent of the total population, though the actual numbers of Christians and Sikhs have been growing over the last few decades.

Of the religions originating in India, the roots of Hinduism stretch back the furthest. Buddhism and Jainism both developed around 500 BC. Buddhism, founded by Siddharta Gautama (who achieved enlightenment and became the Buddha), spread rapidly in the north and over the Himalaya in the two centuries after his death. The Buddhist emperor Asoka spread Buddhism wherever he extended his empire, including Sri Lanka. Hinduism gradually reasserted its hold on the sub-continent, however, and by Independence there were only half a million Buddhists left. The mass conversion to Buddhism of three million *harijans*, following the example of Dr. B.R. Ambedkar, one of the architects of the Constitution, in 1956 was an important political gesture against caste and untouchability. As a consequence, 85 per cent of Indian Buddhists live in Maharashtra, and the remainder in Arunachal Pradesh, Sikkim and the Ladakh district.

Entrance to a Hindu temple, Bhubeneswar.

Hinduism

'Let me proclaim the valiant deeds of Indra,
the first he did, the wielder of the thunder,
when he slew the dragon and let loose the waters,
and pierced the bellies of the mountains.'

Extract from a hymn in the Rig Veda, composed between 1500 and 900 BC and the oldest religious text of Hindus.

From its earliest forms – probably involving the worshipping of a variety of nature gods some 3000 years ago – Hinduism has evolved to become less a single theology than a whole religious world. The most enduring fact of Hinduism is its variety and difference. Reincarnation, for example, is a basic belief of Hinduism, but there are many Hindus in the south who believe in one life only.

Hinduism's holy books, the Bhagavad Gita, the epic Mahabharata, the Ramayana, and the older vedic scriptures, outline through stories, poems and epics the activities of the gods and their relationship to humans. They also outline some of the basic practices of Hinduism such as *puja* (which simply means 'worship') and the rules and regulations of the caste system. The concept of reincarnation is important for many Hindus. A person is reincarnated over and over again until she or he finally achieves *moksha*, which is freedom from births, and spiritual salvation. The *atman* (the immortal principle of the self) is liberated from the body and joins the Brahman – or God. The way in which you live in each life determine how many lives will be needed to attain *moksha*.

Hinduism is also characterised by a pantheon of gods and goddesses. Yet most Hindus will explain that these deities are aspects of one God who has three manifestations: Brahma, the creator, Vishnu the preserver, and Shiva, the destroyer. Most big Hindu temples are dedicated either to Vishnu or Shiva. Some Hindu households have their own household gods to whom they daily perform *puja*. Throughout India small temples and shrines have been built everywhere, sometimes centred on a tree, a termite mound, a snake hole or special stone.

A NATION OF VILLAGES

India is a nation of villages, some 578,000 of them. Some are tiny hamlets, and others, in rich agricultural areas, more like small towns .The density of villages is greater in some parts of India than others. Kerala, for example, with a population of twenty-nine million has only 1,219 villages; Madhya Pradesh with a population only twice as big has well over 70,000 villages, reflecting the fact that Madhya Pradesh has about eleven times more land than Kerala.

Rural India and agriculture are nearly synonymous; with the exception of a few 'service' castes (barber, blacksmith and so on), to live in a village means to depend on farming for a living. Yet the average farmer tills a tiny plot of land, often as little as one acre. Half of the land holdings in India are classified as belonging to what are called 'marginal' farmers, because they have so little land. Only 4 per cent of farmers have over 10 hectares. When farmers have such small farms from which to make a living, it is not surprising that the per capita income in the countryside is less than half the urban one.

Indian villages are generally badly off in terms of development. Electricity, running water, medical facilities, good communications, employment, education and housing are more likely to be in short supply. Literacy among men in villages is half that found in towns; the number of babies who die in their first year almost twice as high. (Urban 65/1000, rural 114/1000.) The Government sees rural development – electrifying villages, building roads and providing schools and health clinics – as one of its most important functions. In the years since Independence many special programmes have been launched to tackle the problems of the countryside.

On the other hand, Indian villages are very lively places. Many village people rarely travel further than they can go on foot, and their village remains the centre of most of their social and economic activity, though each village is firmly linked into regional economic and political life. The pace of life is still determined by the speed of a bullock cart (and India has 13 million bullock carts compared to 88,700 tractors). The year, as in pre-twentieth century English villages, revolves around the growing season, with each point in the agricultural cycle marked with village celebrations and festivals. Ploughing and harvesting are important village events. Families hold their own celebrations to mark major events such as marriage and the birth of children. India's special art of celebration lives on in the villages. Economic poverty is by no means an indication of poverty in other areas of life. Many village people still live in extended families with grandparents, aunts, uncles and cousins under one roof, providing support, stability and a sense of belonging.

'Only that village is fit to live in which has a money lender from whom to borrow in need, a doctor to treat illness, a priest to minister to the soul and a stream that does not dry up in summer.'
Old Sanskrit Text.

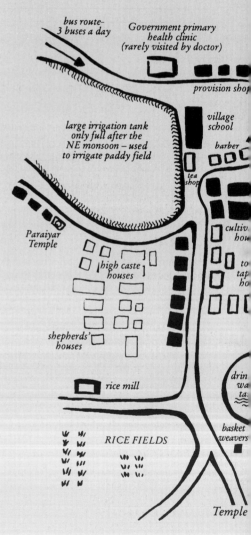

Toddy-tapper drawing off sap from a Palmira palm. This is then either fermented to make an alcoholic drink, or boiled down to make sugar.

John Ogle/Oxfam

bus stand

arket area
shepherds'
houses

oil crusher

Ganesh Temple

washer
family
house

washing tank –
people, animals
and clothing

RICE FIELDS

yanar
mple

Palmira Palms,
source of toddy,
for drinking or
sugar-making

Harijan Colony –
five different
Harijan castes

RICE FIELDS

THE STORY OF A VILLAGE

Inthavur is a village of about 1,500 people not far from the coast in Tamil Nadu. There are fifteen different castes in the village and members of each caste group tend to live close together within the village. There is also a *harijan* colony at a slight distance from rest of the village.

Most of the village families are farmers, and the total area cultivated by the village is about 1200 hectares. The main crop is rice, and during the growing season the village seems to float in a sea of bright green paddy. Higher caste households tend to have the most land and most of the *harijan* castes have none at all. Land is classified into 'wet', because it is watered from the village irrigation tank, and 'dry' because it is too far from the tank and relies only on rainfall. Wet land is used for growing rice, and dry land grows millet, lentils, red chillies, sesame seeds and coriander. When the monsoon is good, the village irrigation tank, which is the size of a large cricket pitch, fills up in just two or three days.

Jyoti is from a *harijan* caste. Her family own no land of their own but are tenant farmers and cultivate about one and a half acres. Instead of paying rent for the fields, they give the landlord a third of everything they harvest. They have two different landlords and, like many other poor families, are at the beck and call of these landlords. This feudal system means that while Jyoti usually gets paid for her work, for other work she just gets a meal. Recently she helped with weeding rice fields for one landlord (paid) and wedding preparations for the other (unpaid). Jyoti supplements her family's meagre income of about Rs2400 a year (£80) by working in the village rice mill. She is given a small portion of each kilo of rice she de-husks as payment.

An important part of village social life is the giving and receiving of small presents at different times of the year, particularly during festivals and family celebrations. Such gifts, often money or food, are always carefully noted down, and an equivalent gift is given back on the next suitable occasion. Rice forms the main village 'currency' as well as being the staple food. Most families eat rice three times a day, sometimes with a vegetable curry, and sometimes just with salt and chillies.

The activities of the year are shaped by the agricultural cycle, which is in turn determined by the rainfall. If one or both of the monsoons fail (which they do perhaps once in four years) there is not enough water to grow rice, and many villagers have a hard time making ends meet. In a year of little rain the village water supply dwindles and dries up by May. Wells are sunk in the bed of the village tanks, but as the water table falls further, women have to walk three or four kilometres to the next village to get water for their families and animals to drink. The harvesting of rice is celebrated by a special festival, Pongal. During Pongal even the animals are given the special celebration food, new rice cooked with milk and brown sugar.

Some of the village families provide important services for other members of the village, either for money or for rice and chillies. Oil-crushing families produce sesame seed oil; migratory shepherds tend herds of goats, leaving them on a different field each night – manure in exchange for rice. There is a barber whose wife is the village midwife; a family of florists who provide flowers (jasmine and marigolds) at festivals; two washer families and a caste of 'toddy tappers' who climb the palm trees that border the rice fields and collect toddy, used to make palm wine. Other families run the tea-shop and the market.

If you fall ill in Inthavur, you have a number of options. You can walk ten kilometres to a primary health centre, or visit one of the village healers. These include a woman who cures dog bites and snake bites; a bone-setter; several herbalists and the village homeopath.

Change is coming to Inthavur; Jyoti's brother-in-law recently moved to Madras where he set up a street stall selling cloth. Jyoti's husband thinks that the family may prosper in a city but Jyoti is not so sure. The family may split, with Jyoti staying in the village as her husband migrates. Such moves strengthen the links between cities and villages, which in turn leads to further change.

WOMEN AT WORK

Women in India share in all the diversity of caste, class and community: the life of a Haryana Muslim women in purdah will be completely different from that of a labouring woman in Andhra Pradesh. Changes since Independence have affected women in different ways. Middle-class women have shared the same boost in income and expectations as middle-class men. A small but highly visible minority of women have achieved considerable advances, professionally and socially. The danger lies in assuming that the lives of all women have improved equally.

Most women in India remain poor, rural and uneducated. Many poor women have two full time jobs: the work they do to earn wages for the family, and the work of running a household. In some rural areas, particularly in the South, poor women work in agriculture; in cities they work in a variety of small-scale industries, or as construction workers, petty traders, and domestic servants. This so called 'informal' sector represents the majority of the work force of India – and particularly women's work – but it is also the area where, according to Ela Bhatt who was a founder member of the Self Employed Women's Association of Ahmedabad (SEWA), the 'grind of work' is overwhelming.

One of the problems for self-employed women is the low pay, long hours and lack of job security they face. There is nobody working on their behalf to improve pay and conditions of work. Many pregnant women work right up to the day they give birth and start work again as little as a week later. Working women often contribute more to the household than anyone else. A study in a rural area of Karnataka in 1981 calculated the amount of energy different members of the household spent on work in a day. It was found that women contributed 53 per cent of the work, men 31 per cent, and children 16 per cent.

SEWA started working with poor women in 1972. By 1989 membership had grown to 29,133. Fruit and vegetable vendors, milk producers, garment stitchers, paper pickers, agricultural workers, and a whole variety of other workers, have come under SEWA's umbrella and successfully demanded better wages and conditions of work. Women vegetable vendors in Ahmedabad, for example, have sold from the same spot for years, but as urban land prices have risen, their spaces have become much sought after. Large merchants and town planners have pressurised the police into arresting and fining vendors just for carrying out their trade. SEWA organised the vendors to demand licences, a process that has taken them to both the Gujarat High Court and the Indian Supreme Court. Now 329 women who sit in the crowded area of Manek Chowk have a legal right to sell their vegetables and cannot be moved on. SEWA has also established its own bank to provide essential financial services to poor women. Training programmes have been set up and women can learn skills as diverse as electrical wiring, fertiliser making and budget preparation.

SEWA is just one example of the transformation that can take place when women themselves organise for change.

'These women are indeed great, as I learn that they are better fighters against poverty than their men, have more calculative, stable, forward looking strategies to deal with their own environment ... The future of the nation lies in the hands of these women.'
Ela Bhatt, National Commission on Self Employed Women and Women in the Informal Sector, 1989.

SEWA market-women on a wet day.

ARRANGED MARRIAGES AND DOWRY

Marriage in India is rarely a private matter between a bride and groom. The vast majority of marriages are 'arranged', usually by senior family members or, among the middle classes, by placing an advertisement in a Sunday paper. Most brides and grooms feel that it is absolutely right that their parents should help in a decision as important as choosing a life partner; some are given the power of veto and may see several prospective partners before they choose. Many, possibly most, arranged marriages lead to happy and stable unions and the so-called 'love marriages' of the West are not looked on as being a particularly desirable alternative.

Dowry on the other hand is universally condemned as a social evil – and universally practised. A dowry is a collection of household items, clothes, jewellery, and money, given at the time of marriage by the parents and relatives of the bride. There is huge social pressure on a family to provide a dowry. Parents fear that their daughter may not be well treated without a dowry, or that they will not be able to find a suitable husband. Even landless labourers are expected to give dowries, which frequently puts them into debt.

Dowry has traditionally been understood as a bride's share of her family's wealth, given at marriage, since once married a woman leaves her family home. Objections to dowry come from the rapid escalation of the size of dowry in the last few decades – it is not uncommon to find a family spending two or three times their annual income – and the recent publicity of the ill-treatment of brides by their in-laws. Escalating dowry demands are often a feature of such ill-treatment, and accounts of 'dowry deaths' are a common feature in national newspapers.

In response to the misery caused by dowry, the Indian women's movement have called for a complete ban: *Dahej mat do, Dahej mat lo* ('Do not give dowry, Do not take dowry'). In 1980, Manushi, a radical women's journal, called on its readers to boycott all weddings which had involved dowry.

However, dowry-giving has shown few signs of diminishing its grip. It has generated much debate in the press; dowry, it is argued, has little, if anything, to do with giving a fair share of the family's wealth to daughters. According to the journalist Madhu Kishwar, it is rather 'a transfer of wealth from men of one family to those of another'. She argues that dowry underlines the subordinate status of women since they are rarely given any control over their own dowry. Dowry is consequently about buying status through a prestigious match, or 'paying' another family to take responsibility for the future of a daughter, since few women are expected to be economically independent. The fact that women work incredibly hard in their new households highlights the irony of a system which sees daughters as a 'burden'. Dowry is one of the clearest signs of a gender role that leaves women's welfare in the hands of men.

Each week in the Sunday papers a few marriage adverts state 'No dowry'. Such marriages are a small but important example that, despite the pressure, it is possible to find a partner in India without giving or receiving a dowry.

Where have all the women gone?

India, unlike most other countries in the world, has fewer women than men. The sex ratio in 1991 was 93 women to every 100 men (UK 106 women per 100 men), compared to a ratio at the beginning of the century of 97 women per 100 men. Extrapolating from the sex ratios in other developing countries, India seems to have 'lost' several million girls and women. Theoretically, females have a better chance of survival than males, but in India it is only when a woman reaches 50 that her life expectancy begins to better that of men. Between birth and the age of nine, far more girl children die, largely from infectious diseases made worse by malnutrition. Maternal mortality takes its toll between the ages of 15 and 34 (500 maternal deaths per 100,000 live births; UK 7 per 100,000). Studies have shown that girls are breast-fed less frequently and for a shorter period than boys; boys are almost always fed before their sisters and sick boys tend to be taken to the doctor sooner than sick girls. This preference for sons is rooted deeply in Indian culture. This is not to say that girl children are not cherished and wanted; the vast majority are. Rather it means that in a country with a population of over 800 million, even a slight bias in favour of sons will have a significant statistical effect.

CHILDREN AT WORK

'... the desire to bloom as a flower
The desire to be a bee to suck honey
The desire to fly like a bird
The desire to flow like a river
The desire to swim like a fish
The desire to shine like a star

Is there no opportunity for all this?'
> Song sung by working children during a campaign in Bangalore
> on the Rights of the Child.

The school at Kuruvikulam.
Julia Mosse/Oxfam

Children have always worked in India. The caste system with its hereditary occupations meant that children helped out with the work of the family and gradually assumed fuller responsibilities. This system of apprenticeship can still be found in India, but it is starting to break down. Nandini Reddy of The Concerned for Working Children, a Bangalore-based organisation, argues that growing poverty has turned children's work into children's labour, as children become their family's main breadwinner; India has the largest work-force of children in the world.

It is almost impossible to calculate the number of children under 15 who work in India today, but estimates vary between 44 million and 100 million or more. Almost 90 per cent of working children are based in rural areas. Children as young as five or six soon learn to take a part in the domestic life of the family, looking after younger children and fetching and carrying firewood and water. Older children tend animals and help with agricultural work. The domestic work of girls is particularly important in rural households, often keeping them from primary school.

This form of work is accepted as a normal part of growing up in India. Nandini Reddy argues that problems arise when children become involved in exploitative sections of the economy, in dangerous occupations, and when they are the family's only earner. Debt, migration, or the death or illness of an adult breadwinner, can turn children into labourers. An estimated three quarters of child labourers are put to work by their parents in situations where the few extra rupees that a child can earn are essential if the family is to stay together. The kind of work that children do varies enormously; they work as petty traders, domestic servants, carpet makers, in the hotel industry, garages and workshops; in hazardous occupations such as the brass industry, firework and match factories, mining, quarrying, and chemical and asbestos factories. Children make for a productive, obedient and effective labour force which is, above all cheap.

The government response to child labour has been selectively to ban it. Ever since 1881 a total ban on child labour has been applied to an increasing number of occupations, although the ban is rarely enforced. As a result, children end up in work which, being illegal, offers them no legal protection, so that a child injured in a work-place accident has no redress through labour law.

An alternative approach to child labour is to protect child workers with minimum wage agreements and adequate working conditions. If child labour were regulated, the argument goes, employers would be forced to stop exploiting children and the advantage of employing them would go. The Concerned for Working Children helped draft legislation passed in 1986 to start this process of regulation, and to ban child labour in 15 hazardous industries. Other people believe that regulating child labour may end up by reinforcing or condoning it. Clearly, the problem needs long-term solutions. Banning it altogether has done little and, as poverty shows no signs of disappearing in India, the problem of child labour is not going to go away on its own.

BASIC INDICATORS
(Based on Government Statistics relating mostly to 1986.)

Population (0-15)	297.4 million
Annual number of births	24.5 million
Infant deaths (0-1 years)	2.4 million
Child deaths (1-4 years)	1.8 million
Still births (estimate)	0.7 million
Infant mortality rate live births	97 per 1000
Percentage of infants with low birth weight	30 per cent
Percentage of malnourished children	40 per cent (approx.)
Children affected by iron-deficiency anaemia	50 per cent (approx.)
Number of children going blind each year due to vitamin A deficiency	40,000 (estimate)

MALARCHI AND THE MATCH-FACTORY CHILDREN

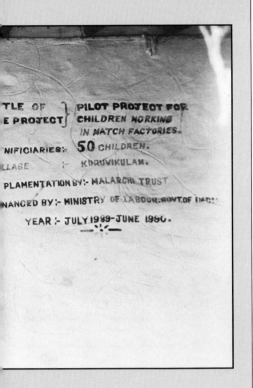

TLE OF | PILOT PROJECT FOR
E PROJECT | CHILDREN WORKING
           IN MATCH FACTORIES.

NIFICIARIES: 50 CHILDREN.

LLAGE : KURUVIKULAM.

PLAMENTATION BY:- MALARCHI TRUST

NANCED BY:- MINISTRY OF LABOUR. GOVT. OF INDI

YEAR :- JULY 1989-JUNE 1990.

Kaliraj is thirteen, though he looks much younger; he is one of five children. He went to school until he was ten, but when his father left home, the family moved from Madurai to Kuruvikulam, about three hours away by bus. Kuruvikulam is one of the match-factory villages of Tamil Nadu. Its factory is situated in an old palace, and every day 2,000 people, mostly children and women, make their living by making matches and match boxes, either in the factory or in their houses in the village. In the shade of every house, women and children fold and stick boxes, their fingers working with a speed that makes the process almost invisible. Kaliraj soon started working in the match factory, putting the match sticks into the metal holders that are dipped in chemicals. His mother and another brother work at home, and another sister goes off at 5 o'clock every morning on a special match-factory bus, to a factory in a neighbouring village. If his mother makes 6,000 outer boxes a day, she earns Rs10 (30p). Each week the factory dispatches 3,960,000 boxes of matches to Delhi and Orissa.

Kaliraj no longer goes to the match factory. Instead, he is going to school again, finishing his education and learning new skills which will provide him with a living other than match-making. He is particularly keen on making wicker furniture; as he says, 'At the match factory I made at the most eight rupees a day; as a furniture maker I'll be able to make at least twenty rupees a day'. Kaliraj's school is one of two pilot projects, run by a group in Tamil Nadu called Malarchi Trust. Malarchi started working with match-factory children almost ten years ago, setting up a number of informal schools for them, usually in the evenings after they finished work. Kaliraj's school is different because it aims to provide a complete alternative to work in a match factory. It starts in the morning, and each pupil gets a stipend of Rs100 a month as well as a good mid-day meal. The Rs100 makes all the difference to parents' willingness to let children stay at school. The prospect of their children learning a more productive skill is equally attractive.

Kaliraj and his friends at the Kuruvikulam school are quite clear about the reasons why children need to work. Jayalaxmi, who is thirteen, lives with her mother and three younger sisters. She explained, 'It was almost impossible at home; we were trying to live on my mother's wages alone; she earned ten rupees in the match factory, and did agricultural work at other times. This is a very dry area, which is why there are so many match factories; it hardly ever rains. So I went to work when I was ten. I was glad to make a contribution to the family; my mother and I worked together to support the family. Now I have started coming to this school, and I can study as well as learning a different trade. If I learn a skill like tailoring, I'll be able to support myself for the rest of my life.'

Malarchi Trust see this school as an important pilot project. They hope the success of their school will encourage the Government to expand the scheme and give other children an alternative to the match factories.

Kaliraj learning to make wicker furniture. He will be able to earn far more as a skilled craftsman than he could as a factory worker.
Julia Mosse/Oxfam

EDUCATION FOR LIFE

Almost every village in India has a primary school, or one within easy reach. Education is free, and in theory, everyone should get at least a primary education. In practice some people fall outside the education system, often because they have to work instead of going to school. Education in schools is only one kind of education, however. There are many groups now working in what is known as 'non-formal education' because it takes place outside the formal education system. Most of the children and adults who participate in non-formal education missed out on the school system, for one reason or another.

Non-formal education has different aims from those of the government schools. One of its objectives is to help people understand their circumstances and their ability to change them. Literacy and practical skills – in health or agriculture, for example – develop as part of a more general learning experience. Small village night schools, where women sit and discuss the problems of the village at the same time as learning to read and write, have sprung up all over India. Non-formal education always builds on the belief that the learners themselves are the richest source for learning. A non-formal approach to telling the time and reading calendars began by discussing the methods of time-keeping that village people already used – looking at the sun, moon and stars and watching the movements of birds and animals. Only when the group appreciated their own methods did they move on to clock and watch reading.

A development group in Bombay helped women pavement dwellers find an alternative to living on pavements. They designed their own houses and planned an entire settlement. At the beginning of the project the women had no idea that they had such abilities. The organisation that helped them, the Society for Promotion of Area Resource Centres (SPARC), saw themselves as 'tourist guides on the voyage of self-discovery' that the women went on.

Sometimes providing non-formal education takes the form of setting up a school for children where there would otherwise be nothing, and designing a curriculum suited to the needs of the children. This was the case for the children who live and work on the rubbish tips of Calcutta.

Young pupils at the school in Dhapa. There are now eight classes and a nursery.

India has a well-developed educational system, with both state and private schools.

AN EDUCATION IN CALCUTTA

There is money to be made from rubbish. On Calcutta's main dumping ground at Dhapa, thousands of families make a living from sorting, selling and recycling the city's waste. Over the years the hillocks of rubbish have rotted down into fertile compost; these are now becoming gardens where vegetables are grown to be sold in the city. In the heart of Dhapa, surrounded by these rubbish heaps, is a school for young garbage pickers. Before the school opened there was no education of any sort for the children of Dhapa. In 1981 the Calcutta Social Project (CSP) held the first non-formal classes with a handful of children out in the open. As the yellow municipal garbage lorries trundled past, the children would rush off to pick over the rubbish, and come back to school when they had finished.

Ten years later the school has flourished. There are now eight classes and a nursery. The school has continued with its non-formal approach, and the children spend time gardening, and learning carpentry, sewing, knitting and chalk making, as well as more usual curriculum activities. Dance and music play an important part in their day. Two sisters from the village of Arupota, beyond the dumps, spoke about the school. Rita is twelve and has been at school for four years. 'Before I came to school, I spent most of my time picking plastic, coal, old tins and that sort of thing. Now I still spend time picking, but I also like reading Bengali. Tagore is my favourite.' Aparana, her younger sister, wants to be a dancer, and is very talented. The school's approach means that she has opportunities both to practise and perform, since every so often the Calcutta Social Project puts on a dance programme in the city.

Manoharpukur is the *basti* (slum) in South Calcutta where CSP first started working. CSP continues to run a non-formal education centre and a health clinic in Manoharpukur. The centre is well used; from early in the morning to late at night, different classes are held for a variety of people. Women's literacy and general education classes, an adult high school covering a formal syllabus, and non-formal classes for school drop-outs, mean that there is something available for anyone who wants to learn. More than 500 people use the centre every day.

Swagata Ghosh is one of the teachers in the centre. She is a dance and music specialist, and comes from a well-known musical family. Why is there such an emphasis in all the CSP schools on dance? She explained, 'When children dance they become receptive, and open to learning other things. Many of the dances are based on the songs of Tagore. This gives them a feel for what is special in their own culture. The children are also very good dancers, which gives them a sense of achievement in circumstances where lots of other things are very hard for them.'

The school amongst the rubbish heaps in Dhapa.

Swagata Ghosh and one of her pupils. Dance offers the children a sense of achievement.

HEALTH FOR ALL?

India's health system sums up all the contradictions of the last 40 years of development. Among the developing countries, India has an impressive and enviable health infrastructure. Some 7,250 Primary Health Centres and 85,000 subcentres (1985 figures) exist in rural areas. Each year well over 12,000 new doctors are trained, along with 8,000 nurses and 5,500 auxiliary nurse-midwives. The ratio of doctors per head of population is well within WHO recommendations and the number of hospital beds grows each year. Treatment and medicines in government hospitals and clinics are free to whoever needs them.

Government provision is only part of the picture. In towns and cities, private health care is a boom industry. Private clinics and hospitals, shops selling a whole spectrum of modern drugs, specialist diagnostic centres and sophisticated 'alternative' therapy centres, are springing up.

Given this two-tier system, which in theory should cover everyone, why do nearly 5 million Indian children die each year from preventable causes? Some estimates claim that only six out of ten Indian children reach adolescence. Why do 1.8 per cent of the population over the age of five have active TB, and many thousands of women die each year because they became pregnant?

Ill health affects poor people far more often than well-off people. As we have seen in other sections, almost half of India's population is below the so-called poverty line. Even if they spend 80 per cent of their total family income on food, they are still not able to buy sufficient calories to feed their families adequately. A child who is malnourished is much more likely to die of an infection such as measles or diarrhoea than a well fed one. A malnourished child is more likely to get sick in the first place.

Despite all the primary health centres in India, only a small proportion of villagers are able to make use of them. Taking time to visit a clinic may be too costly for a working woman because time away from the fields may mean the loss of a day's wages. Bus fares are a luxury; the health centre may be badly stocked or will only give three days' worth of medicine at a time. Referral to a city hospital is both expensive and time-consuming. As a consequence, many poor families continue to use indigenous medical systems unless someone is dying; but by then, trying to find a way around the system of clinics and hospitals is complicated, confusing and often unsuccessful.

Meanwhile, children continue to die. The burden of mortality falls on the shoulders of India's youngest and poorest. Such deaths are interpreted as in some way 'natural' by many Indian families. 'Baur to girta hi hai', they will say, 'blossoms will always fall'.

The groups who are working with poor people to try and improve their health care refuse to accept such deaths as natural. Standard health-care measures such as immunisation and nutritional programmes have an important place but need to be provided in a context of broader social change. Otherwise, health programmes can simply increase the dependency and powerlessness of the people to whom they are offered.

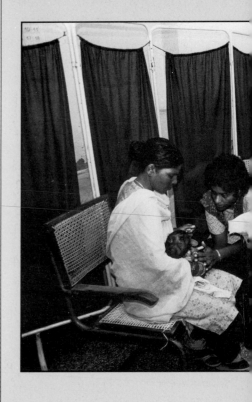

Chandrakala (centre) working in the laboratory attached to the clinic at Dokur. Her ambition is to train to become a doctor.

A BAREFOOT PATHOLOGY LABORATORY

This mother has brought her children to the local clinic for a health check.

Chandrakala works in a pathology laboratory with a difference; it is tucked away in the small village of Dokur, about 100 kilometres from Hyderabad, the capital of Andhra Pradesh. She herself comes from the village, and has studied up to the equivalent of GCSE. Now she divides her time between further studies and her work in the laboratory which is attached to the primary health clinic in her village. The clinic is open daily and Chandrakala has learned how to carry out sputum tests for tuberculosis, blood tests for malaria and routine urine analysis to detect a variety of different conditions. The equipment and chemicals she uses are available locally and, most importantly, don't rely on electricity, since there are frequent power cuts. The village people of Dokur now have an effective and cheap diagnosis service for a range of common health problems, saving a costly trip into town.

The laboratory and clinic at Dokur were set up by the Institute for Rural Health Studies, started in Hyderabad by two women scientists in 1981. One of the aims of the Institute is to carry out research on rural health problems. The research done so far has shown the extent to which these may not be simply 'medical' problems, but part of a broader picture of poverty and lack of resources. One of their earliest studies looked at the effect that easy access to credit had on health. They found that State Bank lending programmes had a dramatic impact on malnutrition among children and adults. The banks lent money to farmers who often used the loans for improving irrigation; this led to added harvests, which increased the work available and improved the wages for agricultural labourers. The knock-on effects reached children and adults alike: because they were better nourished, their general health and well-being improved. The bankers told the Institute that this was the first piece of statistical evidence to show the impact of credit programmes on health and nutrition. As a result, the State Bank plans to extend the programme throughout the State – which should result in better nutrition levels and health for more village people.

The Institute is also studying ways of improving health care delivery. This is where Chandrakala comes in. The Institute set up two clinics with laboratories to find out whether village people will use local health care facilities, if they believe these are adequate, rather than travel further afield. The first of these clinics now draws patients from 25 villages in the area. Another attraction of the clinics is their referral systems. At Dokur, Chandrakala works with a trained paramedic, Hanumantha Rao, who visits the clinic for one or two weeks each month. Chandrakala refers problem cases to him, and he in turn takes serious cases to visit a competent specialist in a nearby city. The fact that villagers know that they will be looked after by a member of the Institute staff and not just abandoned to the workings of the urban medical system has increased their willingness to use the clinics.

Chandrakala loves her work in the laboratory and cherishes a dream of one day becoming a doctor and working with poor people in rural areas. The third member of the team in Dokur is Raju. Raju was badly affected by an attack of polio but has been treated through the Institute. Now he dispenses medicines and keeps the records.

The clinic at Dokur offers a model of effective health care in the hands of local people. Together with the Institute's work on the causes of ill health, it points to new and more effective ways of tackling the health care of India's millions of rural poor. The health secretary of Andhra Pradesh – a state with some 66 million people – has asked the Institute to set up an identical facility in its model health area so that it can evaluate the effectiveness of the scheme. The acting director of the Institute explains, 'Rural village clinics have been shown to be a cost effective way of providing health care and thus assuring that health for all is not just rhetoric but reality for rural people.'

AN URBAN EXPLOSION

India has one of the world's most rapidly expanding urban populations. The twelve largest cities were, on average, 45 per cent bigger in 1981 than they were in 1971 (except Bangalore, which had grown by 77 per cent in the same period). Calcutta, India's largest city, has already passed the ten million mark, and Bombay, Delhi and Madras are all expected to have upwards of ten million citizens by the year 2000. Some estimates suggest they may be almost there already. It is not just the metropolitan centres that are growing; villages are turning into towns and smaller towns are growing into bigger ones. Meanwhile agricultural land is eaten up by growing cities; an estimated 1.5 million hectares (an area the size of Northern Ireland) have disappeared under urban sprawl since 1950.

Why are the cities growing? Apart from their own natural growth rate, India's cities attract labourers who migrate from the countryside. Cities offer higher wages, more regular work, and access to a health and education system. A study in Delhi showed that migrant workers earned two and a half times more than they could have earned in the same period in their villages. Migrant labourers stay in the only place that is available to them, swelling the shanty towns. The Planning Commission estimates that 20 per cent of the urban population live in slums; others put the estimate higher.

Moving to a city is usually a carefully worked out strategy. When people move to cities they stay in touch with their relatives back home. Contrary to myths about millions of unemployed 'hangers on', new arrivals to the city, aided by their relatives and friends, rarely stay out of work for long. India's growing middle-classes and the expanding service sector generate a hungry demand for workers – for domestic servants, builders, hotel workers, rickshaw drivers, and petty traders who carry everything from vegetables to carpets around the middle-class housing areas. People from slums provide many of the services that sustain the life style of the middle classes, and most regard themselves as having made a positive choice in moving from the villages. Far from traditional life styles breaking down in slums, family relationships, festivals and marriages knit communities together, provide continuity and stabilise family life. Living in a slum may be hard work, but slum families show enormous resilience, skill and energy.

For many years local and national governments tried to evict slum dwellers and bulldoze their huts, since they were classified as illegal squatters. In the last decade the fruitlessness of this approach has become apparent. Quite clearly, migrant families make an important contribution to the economic life of cities, and they need homes. The new strategy, beginning to gain acceptance, is to let slums stay but to upgrade them, to provide an infrastructure in the form of sanitation, water, health services and schools.

This process has taken place more successfully in some cities than in others. In Hyderabad many slum dwellers have been granted ownership rights to their house plots, a move which has led to a high degree of involvement and self-help in efforts to improve slums. Unfortunately, at the moment slums are growing faster than the government's ability to upgrade them. As a result, millions of slum dwellers remain in poor huts in crowded, often unhealthy conditions. But city life offers an attractive alternative to rural unemployment and, above all, the hope that things will be better for one's children.

Contrasting styles of architecture in Calcutta.

A LIVING FROM THE CITY

As Delhi expanded, it swallowed up many of the surrounding villages. Fifty years ago, Chandravati B lived in one of these villages. 'I used to cut grass for a living', she said, 'After a while, there was no more grass to cut, only streets and houses.'

Chandravati B became a widow when she was only 20. Her husband was shot while he was taking part in a Home Rule demonstration near the Red Fort in Delhi. She suddenly found herself without any means of support and with a child to look after. 'My life has been very hard work; I spent 30 years bending down to cut grass. It was often wet, and carrying it on my head gave me terrible backache.' As her village became a suburb, finding the grass to cut became more difficult; having no other skills she found it hard to make ends meet until she was offered a training in traditional Indian crafts by the SMM Theatre Crafts Trust, which had opened a workshop, called Naika, near the area that was once her village. 'I came knowing nothing; now I can make almost anything – horses, dolls, elephants, masks and puppets. In 22 years I've turned my hand to just about everything.'

The SMM Theatre Crafts Trust was established by a woman called Kamaladevi Chattopadhyay, who was dedicated to keeping alive Indian crafts. 'Though not an artisan myself,' she wrote, 'I represent those who love and cherish crafts, and are deeply interested in and concerned about their future.' Naika trained 200 local women in theatre crafts, including Chandravati B, and offered craftsmen and women from all over India an opportunity to work on their crafts with a regular income and support from the Trust.

One of these craftswomen was Chandravati A (as she is called at Naika to avoid confusion with Chandravati B!). She is the master of the papier-mache section, a central role since many crafts use papier-mache as a base. She comes from a family of papier-mache workers, but she is the last one of the family to make her living from the craft. She sat shaping a trunk for the elephant-headed god Ganesh: 'I've worked with this since I was a child, making gods and goddesses for different festivals. When my husband died I had a family of six to take care of, and for a while we had nothing to eat. One of my relatives was already working at Naika and so I came here too. That was about 20 years ago. I'm paid a good salary and I'm happy to be able to practise my skill.'

Oxfam's trading division, Bridge, buys crafts from Naika to sell in Britain. Many of the workers were busy making bird carousels for the Christmas catalogue. Regular orders from Bridge form a dependable part of Naika's income, which means that they can keep a team of 55 craftspeople, mostly women, employed all the year round. Other income comes from selling crafts in Naika's shop, and from special commissions for festivals and conferences. Naika was involved in preparations for the Festival of India, for example.

For Chandravati A and Chandravati B, both poor women faced with the dilemma of earning a living in a city, there is considerable satisfaction in working on traditional crafts. 'One has to work', said Chandravati B, 'and this work is much better than most. I am very content.'

Chandravati A making papier-mache models of Ganesh, the elephant-headed god, and Chandravati B at work in the craft workshop.

WORKING WITH THE POOR

India's Non-Governmental Organisations

Non-governmental organisations (or NGOs) are groups of people working for change all over the world. NGOs in India started with missionary and charity work in the British period, and the growing nationalist movement, the influence of Gandhi, and the emergence of radical politics in the 1960s led to the formation of many hundreds (now thousands) of organisations working with poor people. Early NGOs tended to be welfare-oriented, setting up orphanages, schools and hospitals. By the 1960s the emphasis shifted towards finding technical solutions, and irrigation, well-digging, and health projects were set up.

Nowadays, instead of 'experts' going into villages and digging wells, NGO workers are more likely to help village people form groups to decide for themselves what changes they need to work for in their own community, looking at issues such as the level of wages, the distribution of land and the way the caste system works. A village group may decide to put up street lighting, open a primary health centre, or set up a credit scheme. This kind of work is often called 'social organisation'.

Recently some NGOs have begun working on specific issues – the environment, working children, rehabilitation of people displaced by large dams, and social forestry are some of the areas in which NGOs are trying to record what is happening in India, and to work for social change. Many NGOs are supported by money from overseas. Oxfam is one among many international donor agencies working in India and works with the people who feature in this book.

Oxfam in India

In 1951, when famine struck Bihar, the recently formed Oxford Committee for Famine Relief began collecting money and clothing for the affected people. By the early 1960s Oxfam had expanded its work in India, supporting welfare projects such as homes for destitute people, and technical training. Oxfam's first field office was opened in Bangalore in 1965 and soon Oxfam was working in almost all the states in India.

Oxfam now has seven field offices, and a coordinating office in Delhi. Each office team is a mixture of field staff who regularly visit the projects funded by Oxfam, and support and administrative staff. Oxfam does not run any projects directly itself, but instead funds NGOs, known as project partners; all the projects that appear in this book are run by Oxfam's project partners. Each office provides its project partners with other kinds of support, organising seminars and workshops on relevant issues, arranging training programmes, and encouraging networking between NGOs.

In the 40 years it has been working in India, Oxfam has learnt that the best form of development is the development of people, and lasting change only comes about when people themselves decide on the changes that they want to bring about, and are given support while they work for these changes. Project partners such as SEWA, GVMAT and TDFF have shown that when people act together they become effective. Soniben, Soosamma, Kaliraj, and all the others whose stories appear in this book, challenge the assumption that poor people cannot change their lives for the better.

Sources and Further Reading

Argawal A., *et al.* (1987), *The Fight for Survival: People's action for environment*, New Delhi: Centre for Science and Environment.

The Second Citizen's Report on the Environment 1987, New Delhi: Centre for Science and Environment.

Argawal, A. and Narain, S. (1989), *Towards Green Villages: A strategy for environmentally-sound and participatory rural development*, New Delhi: Centre for Science and Environment.

(1987), *A Social and Economic Atlas of India*, Delhi: Oxford University Press.

Argawal, A.N., Varma, H.O., and Gupta, R.C. (1989), *India Economic Information Yearbook, 1989-1990*, New Delhi: National Publishing House.

Bhatt, E. (1989), *Grind of Work*, Ahmedabad: Self Employed Women's Association.

Biardeau, M. (1989), *Hinduism: The anthropology of a civilization*, Oxford: Oxford University Press.

Butler, D., Lahiri, A., and Roy, P. (1989), *India Decides: Elections 1952-1989*, New Delhi: Living Media Books.

Gupte, P. (1989), *India: The challenge of change*, London: Methuen.

Jain, L.C., Krishnamurthy B.V. and Tripathi, P.M. (1985), *Grass without Roots: Rural development under government auspices*, New Delhi: Sage Publications.

Jeffery, P., Jeffery, R., and Lyon, A. (1988), *Labour Pains and Labour Power: Women and childbearing in India*, London: Zed Books.

Maliekal, J. (1979), *The Independence Movement*, Bangalore: Centre for Social Action.

Mukhopadhyay, M. (1984), *Silver Shackles: Women and development in India*, Oxford: Oxfam.

Nandy, A. (1983), *The Intimate Enemy: Loss and recovery of self under colonialism*, New Delhi: Oxford University Press.

Overseas Development Institute (1989), *Briefing Paper: India's economy after the elections*, London: ODI.

Shiva, V. (1988), *Staying Alive: Women, ecology and survival in India*, London: Zed Books.

Spear, P. (1978), *A History of India Volume 2: From the sixteenth century to the twentieth century*, London: Penguin Books.

Thapar, R. (1966), *A History of India, Volume 1: From the discovery of India to 1526*, London: Penguin Books.

World Bank (1990), *World Development Report, 1990*, Oxford: Oxford University Press.